Praise for

*Praying the Scriptures
for Your Teens*

Don't miss out on praying these Scriptures for your teens. It is the greatest gift you can give them. It will change their lives!

Fern Nichols, president,
Moms in Prayer International (formerly Moms In Touch)

You'll laugh, cry, and identify with Jodie. She's real. Best of all, these pages will give you a strategy and a hope.

Susan Alexander Yates,
author of *And Then I Had Teenagers*
and *31 Days of Prayers for My Teen*

This is an easy to use yet incredibly effective guide for parents who want to use to the fullest the two most powerful tools in parenting—prayer and Scripture.

Joe White, president,
Kanakuk Kamps

Also by Jodie Berndt

Celebration of Miracles

Praying the Scriptures for Your Children

PRAYING
the Scriptures
for Your
TEENS

Discover How to Pray God's
Purpose for Their Lives

JODIE BERNDT

We want to hear from you. Please send your comments about this
book to us in care of zreview@zondervan.com. Thank you.

ZONDERVAN

Praying the Scriptures for Your Teens
Copyright © 2007 by Jodie Berndt

This title is also available as a Zondervan ebook.
Visit www.zondervan.com/ebooks.

Requests for information should be addressed to:

Zondervan, *Grand Rapids, Michigan 49530*

Library of Congress Cataloging-in-Publication Data

Berndt, Jodie.
    Praying the Scriptures for your teenagers : discover how to pray God's will for
their lives / Jodie Berndt.
        p. cm.
    Includes bibliographical references and index.
    ISBN 978-0-310-27351-6
    1. Mothers — Prayer-books and devotions — English. 2. Christian teenagers —
Religious life. 3. Bible — Devotional literature. I. Title.
BV4847.B46   2007
248.3'2085 — dc22
                                                  2006100428

Cover photography: Veer®
Interior design: Beth Shagene

Printed in the United States of America

HB 05.16.2017

For Hillary, Annesley, Virginia, and Robbie —

I have no greater joy than to hear
that my children are walking in the truth.
3 JOHN 4

I love you.

Contents

PART 1: PRAYING for Your TEEN'S CHARACTER

PART 2: PRAYING for Your TEEN'S RELATIONSHIPS

PART 3: PRAYING for Your TEEN'S HEALTH and SAFETY

PART 4: PRAYING for Your TEEN'S VICTORY over TEMPTATION

PART 5: PRAYING for Your TEEN'S FUTURE

Foreword

If you have teens — and if you picked up this book, my guess is that you do — I don't have to tell you that there is a battle going on. As parents, we can be easily tempted to believe that the fight is with our kids. But as we look around at what the world has to offer — from point-and-click pornography, to television and movies dripping with violence and sex, to music that pulses with obscenity and anger — we cannot help but realize that our battle is not *against* our teens; it is *for* them.

My wife, Katie, and I have three children. We know, as you do, that raising teens is an immense responsibility, a terrific honor, and a downright heartrending job. Watching our kids grow, test their boundaries, and step out on their own — making good decisions and bad ones — demands an amazing kind of love. One of the best ways we can express this love is through prayer.

Several years ago, Katie and I began praying God's Word over our children. We have found this approach to be effective and productive — particularly during those times when our own words, or our own attempts to pursue and protect our kids, were not enough. In this book, Jodie Berndt captures the spirit of those prayers. Using real stories of real struggles, she gives parents a platform for understanding, applying, and strategically using God's Word.

In my work with Teen Mania, I have the privilege of being with—and praying for—teens every single day. I see their hurts, their frustrations, and the challenges they face. I see the battle raging, and I am consumed by the call to capture their hearts, to renew their minds, and to see their shattered lives healed and restored *now*.

My prayer is that you, too, will be consumed by the call. May this book—and the power that comes through praying the Scriptures—challenge, equip, and inspire you as you step onto the battlefield and pursue God's will for your children and your family.

> RON LUCE,
> founder and president
> of Teen Mania

Acknowledgments

Imagine how you'd feel if someone asked you all sorts of personal questions about your teen—and then took your answers and put them into a book, in unvarnished black and white, for all the world to see.

Raising teens—and praying for them—is not an easy job. Even when God is obviously working in a teen's life, we parents tend to hold our breath, knowing that—to put a new twist on an old song—tomorrow (and the uncertainty it holds) is only a day away. I'll say more on this subject in the introduction, but for now I want to extend a huge and heartfelt thank you to all of those—from my dearest friends to complete strangers like the mother I met outside the gates of a Christian summer camp—who were bold enough, vulnerable enough, and faith-filled enough to share their stories with me. In return for your gift, I'm asking God to "throw open the floodgates of heaven and pour out so much blessing" on your families that you will not be able to contain it![1]

I also want to express appreciation to—and admiration for—the very talented team of editors, designers, and marketing professionals at Zondervan. The company's motto, *Live Life Inspired*, seems a fitting description for the way that these

---

1. Malachi 3:10.

folks approach their jobs, and I am deeply grateful to Sandy Vander Zicht, Dirk Buursma, and Jamie Hinojosa for how they have equipped and inspired me to do mine. As you continue to proclaim God's love to a world in need, "may the Lord our God show you his approval and make your efforts successful."[1]

Finally, to my husband, Robbie, and to the four people we pray for the most—Hillary, Annesley, Virginia, and Robbie—you are amazing. I *love* the many ways that I see Jesus and his kingdom work reflected in your lives. My prayer for you is that "your love may abound more and more in knowledge and depth of insight, so that you may be able to discern what is best and may be pure and blameless until the day of Christ, filled with the fruit of righteousness that comes through Jesus Christ—to the glory and praise of God."[2]

To you, Lord God, be the glory!

Everything that was written in the past
was written to teach us, so that through endurance
and the encouragement
of the Scriptures we might have hope.

ROMANS 15:4

---

1. Psalm 90:17 NLT.   2. Philippians 1:9–11.

Introduction

"If you remain in me and my words remain in you,
ask whatever you wish, and it will be given you."

JOHN 15:7

As I was working on this book, the folks at Zondervan emailed to let me know that they were having a meeting about the cover design. Did I, they asked, have any specific ideas or input to contribute?

"Well," I said, "if you were to poll my friends who are raising teens right now, they'd probably tell you to just go ahead and make the cover black."

"Black?"

"Yes, but you could put a ray of light cutting across the darkness to symbolize God's intervention in our desperate lives."

When my mother heard my suggestion, she balked. "A black cover? That's a pretty far cry from the beautiful garden gate on the front of *Praying the Scriptures for Your Children*."

13

"Yes, it is," I agreed. "But believe me, as a mother of teens, my prayers are a pretty far cry from where they were when I wrote that book."

I wasn't really serious about using a black cover—who'd want to buy it?—but the truth of the matter is that we parents of teens *are* in a different place, prayer-wise. We still want our kids to develop godly characters and have a strong, vibrant faith—but now that they are older, we have a whole new list of prayer needs, some of which are literally life-and-death issues. Safety on the road, eating disorders, drug and alcohol use, sexual purity—concerns like these can turn a tidy little prayer journal into a minefield faster than you can say, "Dear God, help!"

The one thing that *hasn't* changed, though, is God's word. If you read *Praying the Scriptures for Your Children*—better yet, if you prayed your way through the book—you know that God's word is powerful and effective. You know that it does not return empty but always accomplishes God's purposes and desires. And, perhaps more than anything else, you know that it holds the key to hope.[1]

And hope, in a nutshell, is what this book is all about.

As a mom, I've always considered prayer a vital part of my job description (as someone once said, "If you're not praying for your child, who is?"), but when I began using Scripture as the basis for my prayers—taking the actual words in the Bible and turning them into prayers—I found that prayer became less of a "duty" and more of an adventure. Reading my Bible, I would discover little nuggets that I could pray over my kids, and my prayer life took on a whole new dimension. Gone were the repetitive and sometimes—dare I say it?—boring petitions for

---

1. Hebrews 4:12; Isaiah 55:11; Romans 15:4.

generic blessings and protection. All of a sudden, my prayers became interesting and creative and infused with a fresh kind of power. I shouldn't have been surprised—after all, Hebrews 4:12 (NLT) tells us that God's word is "alive and powerful"—but I wasn't prepared for the depth of fulfillment, joy, and confidence that came with tapping into principles and promises that had first sprung from the heart of Almighty God!

My desire, in writing this book, is to give you that same sense of confidence and joy. I've arranged the chapters topically; feel free to flip around as you pray your way through the various seasons in your teen's life. At the end of each chapter, you'll find several Bible verses written in the form of prayers. You can pick just one of these verses, or pray your way through all of them, switching the "he/she" pronouns around for your son or your daughter as needed. Once you find out what's here, you can dig around in your own Bible for additional verses, or just keep this book on your nightstand as a "reference manual" for those times when you want a prayer verse in a hurry. (I'll never forget the time that, needing a few quick verses to pray about a particular concern, I picked up my bedside copy of *Praying the Scriptures for Your Children*. Our daughter Virginia came into the room, took one look, and laughed out loud. "You're reading your own book?" she teased. "Mom, that's just so *sad!*" Little did she know that I was using the prayer verses on her behalf!)

In the coming pages, you'll meet parents who have wrestled and grappled and prayed their way through everything from their teen's questions about God to issues like loneliness, anger, parties, and relationships. You'll meet teens—musicians and athletes, popular kids and loners, churchgoers and rebels—

and see how God has worked in their lives. And although I have often changed names or small details to protect their identities, all of the people in this book are real.

They are also people who know that God is not finished with them yet. Not one of the moms and dads I talked with would claim to have a corner on good parenting, or good praying. They know — as I do — that when God delivers their teen from the concern or crisis *du jour*, the next one might be only a history class, or a party, or a boyfriend away.

If we know nothing else, we can be sure that teens' lives will be full of surprises.

If you want to know the truth, this reality — that our teens are still under construction — served as a bit of a stumbling block for some parents. Knowing that their kids were probably not out of the woods, trouble-wise, and that they almost certainly had hurdles yet to cross, some folks were reluctant to discuss the good things that God had done in their families, lest they appear to be counting their chickens too soon. Not only that, but one mother I spoke with worried that if she talked about what God had done in her daughter's life — the answers to prayer that she had experienced — it might look as though she was being boastful.

As I was wondering about these concerns — and about whether, given folks' reticence, I would even have enough material to sustain a book — God spoke to my heart as clearly as I have ever heard him. He directed me to 1 Samuel 7, the passage where the threat of a Philistine assault has the Israelites shaking in their boots. "Do not stop crying out to the LORD our God for us," the Israelites beg Samuel, "that he may rescue us from the hand of the Philistines" (verse 8).

Samuel prays, God answers, and the Israelites wind up slaughtering the bad guys. Afterward, Samuel takes a stone and sets it up not far from the battlefield. He names the stone "Ebenezer"—which literally means "stone of help"—saying, "Thus far has the LORD helped us" (verse 12).

If you know anything about Israel's history, you know that the Philistines were a constant source of trouble. The Israelites had been battling them on and off for years before Samuel came on the scene, and then for years afterward—they are the guys who produced Goliath, the defiant giant whose death catapulted David into the national spotlight. When Samuel set up his Ebenezer stone, he certainly had no illusions that the Philistines had been banished forever.

But did that stop him from thanking God, or from giving him public glory? Not at all! Samuel set up the stone as a marker—a sign of remembrance—so that in the years and generations to come, all of Israel would be able to look at it and say, "Thus far has the LORD helped us."

As praying parents, this is the attitude that we need to take. Rather than cowering in worry or fear over the Philistines that lurk around our next corner, we need to stop and thank God for what he has already done in our teens' lives. When God works in answer to our prayers, we need to raise our own Ebenezers, giving him credit and honor for what he has done "thus far"—and knowing that he will be there for us in the future.

The verse at the beginning of this introduction—John 15:7—says that if we remain in Christ and his words remain in us, we can ask whatever we wish, and it will be given us. That's a beautiful promise, but it's only part of the story. In the very next verse, Jesus explains why this arrangement even matters: "This is to my Father's glory," he says, "that you bear much fruit, showing yourselves to be my disciples."

As you read the stories in this book—and as you put your teen's name in the prayers at the end of each chapter—you can do so knowing that you are bringing glory and honor to God. Yes, you and your family will reap the rewards of your prayers—that's part of how we bear fruit and prove that we are Christ's disciples. But that's not the most important thing. The most important thing is that God will be glorified.

Only God would think of using *teens* to do that!

PART 1

PRAYING
for Your **TEEN'S**
CHARACTER

CHAPTER 1

Praying for Honesty and Integrity

The LORD detests lying lips,
but he delights in those who tell the truth.
Proverbs 12:22 NLT

"Where were you last night?"

Molly eyed her daughter, watching carefully for any hint of deception. Her maternal instincts had kicked into overdrive, but she wanted to give Jenna a chance to tell the truth before she confronted her with what she already knew: that Jenna had left a birthday party and then shown up — much later — at a girlfriend's house where she had been invited to spend the night.

"I was at Allie's house."

"How did you get there?"

"Brian drove me there after the party."

Molly had never heard Jenna talk about anyone named "Brian," but she had heard — from another mom — that Jenna had left the birthday party with a boy.

"Who's Brian?" Molly asked.

"He's a friend of Allie. He offered to take me to her house."

"Did you kiss him?"

"Mom! What's with all the questions?"

Molly hadn't planned to ask about the kissing; the question had simply popped into her head. And now that Jenna had sidestepped the issue, she sensed that she had hit a mark.

"Did you kiss Brian?" she repeated.

"No, Mom!" Jenna scoffed. "*Nothing* happened!"

There it was: the slightest cloud that flickered across Jenna's face, signaling to Molly that her daughter was not telling the truth. Molly didn't really care whether or not Jenna had kissed anyone; that wasn't the issue. It was the lying about it that mattered—and lately, it seemed, Jenna had been lying about a lot of things. She lied about what she ate; she lied about whose clothing she wore. She even lied about things that didn't make any sense—like when she told a friend that she had broken a picture frame, when Molly knew that she hadn't!

Later that night, Molly turned to her prayer journal. She flipped back through the pages, her eyes scanning the prayers she had written during the past few months:

Write your word on Jenna's heart, that she would choose to hate sin and love your holiness. The words were based on Psalm 119:9–11. *Gather the wheat in Jenna's life, and burn up the chaff.* Luke 3:17. *Before a word is on her tongue, you know it completely, Lord. Shine your light on the darkness in her life, and lead her in the way everlasting.* A few verses from Psalm 139.

As Molly reread the prayer, she realized that she was exhausted. "Father," she prayed, "I am too tired to fight this battle. If Jenna is not telling the truth about kissing Brian, I am going to let it go—but I am trusting you to work in her life and to smash the spirit of lying that is trying to take up residence in her heart."

The prophet Jeremiah would have understood Molly's fatigue, as well as her heartache. Way back when he was a teen, about six hundred years before Jesus was born, deception was evidently a way of life among God's people. "Beware of your neighbor!" the prophet warned. "Beware of your brother! They all take advantage of one another and spread their slanderous lies. They all fool and defraud each other; no one tells the truth. With practiced tongues they tell lies; they wear themselves out with all their sinning. They pile lie upon lie and utterly refuse to come to [God]."[1]

With practiced tongues they tell lies.

There's no question that lying gets easier with practice and that our teens are growing up in a world where kids learn to deny guilt, shift blame, withhold information, twist the truth, break promises, and even tell straight-up, bold-faced lies — often without even blinking. We might think that this sort of blatant deception is a modern problem, but consider the fact that Cain, history's very first teen, lied to God — *to God!* — after he had murdered his brother. "Where is he?" God wanted to know. "I don't know!" Cain retorted. "Am I supposed to keep track of him wherever he goes?"[2]

When teens lie, it's often for the same reasons that adults do: to impress people, to advance themselves (academically, financially, or in some other way), to protect their friends, and — like Cain — to get out of trouble. While these reasons may make a lie *understandable*, they should never make lying *acceptable*. God doesn't wink at deception. Not only did he put lying

1. Jeremiah 9:4–6 NLT.   2. See Genesis 4:8–10 NLT.

on his Top Ten list in the Old Testament, but at the end of the New Testament he lumps liars with cowards, murderers, sorcerers, and a host of other vile creatures, saying that their place will be in "the fiery lake of burning sulfur."[1] And — just in case we need some cake with that icing — he punctuates the rest of the Bible with such words as "hate," "detest," and "abhor" to describe how he feels about dishonesty.[2] And why wouldn't God feel this way? Where, after all, do lies come from? From Satan — the one Jesus called "the father of lies"![3]

Peggy is a mom who places a high priority on honesty. She taught her kids that omitting details from a story was the same thing as lying, and she prayed that if they were ever doing anything wrong, they would be caught. She also prayed that they would *always* tell the truth, no matter what.

Little did Peggy know what would happen when God answered those prayers ...

Crash!

The can of soda smashed through the window, spilling its contents onto the living room floor. Car wheels drowned out the sound of the boys' laughter as they sped away. As members of their high school's championship soccer team, they were all too familiar with late-night pranks, and this latest — a stealth attack on the home of their archrival's leading scorer — seemed, in their adolescent minds, to be a brilliant idea.

When Peggy learned that her son, Charlie, had participated in the vandalism, she took a different view. "It was a definite

---

1. Exodus 20:16; Revelation 21:8.   2. See, for instance, Psalm 5:6; Proverbs 6:16–17; 12:22.
3. John 8:44.

moment of stupidity," she said. "The boys had planned to put Oreos on this other fellow's car as a practical joke, and the prank got out of hand."

But that was just the beginning. Called into the school office the next day, the boys learned that they had been caught on videotape as they purchased their arsenal of soda and cookies. "Do you want to tell me about it?" the school official asked.

To a man, the other culprits—all considered "team leaders" by their coach and the other players—denied any wrongdoing. Charlie, though, could not keep silent. As an honor student and a well-known leader in his church youth group, he felt that he needed to confess. He had no interest in staging any sort of a cover-up, and he fully believed Jesus' words in John 8:31–32: "If you hold to my teaching, you are really my disciples. Then you will know the truth, and the truth will set you free." Charlie had made a mistake; now all he wanted was to set the record straight and make amends.

"You're crazy!" one of his teammates cried, when he learned what Charlie had done.

"What were you thinking?" asked another. "We need to stick together. If you hadn't confessed, they never would have been able to prove we had anything to do with what happened!"

Never before had Charlie so keenly felt the pain of rejection. But as it turned out, his teammates' ire was the least of his worries. The man whose house the boys had damaged was not about to settle matters quietly. Rather than accept payment for his broken window and soiled carpet, he decided to go to court—and in the end, Peggy and her husband wound up shelling out more than $10,000 in lawyer and court fees.

Not only that, but Charlie's conviction—all but assured by his confession—went on his permanent record and, in addition to having to perform 250 hours of community service and attend six months' worth of youth offender classes, the judge ruled that Charlie had to spend three days in jail!

"I cannot begin to tell you the pain I felt having to watch my son walk into that jail," Peggy said. "As the gates shut behind him, locking him in with a bunch of felons, I felt like all my dreams for him were shattered. I knew that his future would never be the same."

And indeed, Charlie's reputation was tarnished. During his college application interview, one of the interviewers pulled up his name on the Internet and discovered that he had been indicted for a felony. After a lengthy explanation, Charlie was accepted at the university—but two years later, when he tried to lease an apartment near the campus, he was turned down, based on the results of a routine criminal background check!

"I never dreamed that telling the truth could be so costly," Peggy said. "But I have discovered that, very often, our greatest growth comes from our greatest failures. Charlie has taken responsibility for his life, and he is mature beyond his years. He has compassion for others, and the grace that he shows is only that of someone who has experienced the grace of God."

"And," she continued, "*I've* learned some lessons, too. I have had to learn how to forgive the man whose desire for vengeance did so much damage to my family. I have learned that just because someone makes a bad decision, they are not a bad person—and they need grace and mercy, rather than condemnation and judgment. Most of all, I have learned that, despite what I sometimes think, I am not in control of my teen's journey toward God—but God is."

Prayer Principle

Very often, our greatest growth comes
from our greatest failures.

Poised for Prayer

Telling the truth can be costly, but holding on to a lie always comes with its own set of—far more dire—consequences. Scripture is full of train-wreck stories about lives gone awry as the result of a lie: Rebekah deceived her husband and—for all practical purposes—lost her favorite son. Jacob lied to his father and had to run for his life. Ananias and his wife lied to the early church about money—and dropped dead on the spot![1]

Stories like these can make us shudder. But if you've caught your teen in a lie, or even if lying seems to be your teen's preferred communication style, don't panic. Instead, try to discover what motivated the lie—Fear? Insecurity? A desire to "cover" for friends?—so that you will be better equipped to pray. Also, keep talking about the importance of truthfulness and integrity, looking at the issue from God's perspective. (My friend Lisa knows that her kids are heaven-bound, but she had them memorize a shortened version of Revelation 21:8—"Liars go to hell"—just to keep them on their toes.)

Remember, too, where lies originate. Satan is the father of lies, and he likes nothing better than to get us to believe his

---

1. Genesis 27; Genesis 29:16–25; Acts 5:1–10.

twisted words. One of the things I liked best about Peggy's story was that she refused to listen to Satan. She could be living in a prison of bitterness, but she chose to forgive the man who hurt her son. She could have seen the entire experience as a tragic mess, but she has chosen to find God's redemptive purposes instead. She could have beaten herself up over her failure to successfully manage her son's life, but she has learned to let God be in control.

What about you? What are the lies that Satan is trying to get you to believe? Has he told you that you have blown it as a parent, and that you will *never* get it right? Has he whispered that your teen is a mess, and that nothing will *ever* change? Don't listen! Don't believe it! Counter lies like these with truths from God's Word: Philippians 1:6 says that God has begun a good work in your child, and that he promises to finish what he starts. If you could talk to Molly, the mom I mentioned at the beginning of this chapter, she'd tell you that God is definitely at work in Jenna's life. Not only did Jenna confess to—and ask forgiveness for—lying about the kiss (Molly's instincts were right!), but in the past year, the shadows of deception have all but disappeared. Today, she and Jenna enjoy a relationship marked by open communication and truthfulness that goes beyond anything Molly could have ever imagined.

Satan may be the father of lies, but Jesus Christ is the Truth. Let's call out to him, trusting in his incomparably great power to change our hearts and set our families free.

Prayers You Can Use

Heavenly Father,

Cause _____ to put off falsehood and speak truthfully to his friends, his teachers, and to us, for we are all members of one body.   EPHESIANS 4:25

Keep _____ from deceitful ways. Teach her to choose the way of truth so that she will never be put to shame. Let her run in the path of your commands, knowing that you have set her heart free.   PSALM 119:29–32

Let _____'s words be truthful, so that they will stand the test of time. Give him a heart that is filled with peace and joy instead of deceit.   PROVERBS 12:19–20

Keep _____'s tongue from evil and her lips from speaking lies, that she may love life and enjoy good days.

PSALM 34:12–13

I know, Lord, that you examine hearts and rejoice when you find integrity there. Let all that _____ does be done with pure motives, and make him always want to obey you. See to it that his love for you never changes.

1 CHRONICLES 29:17–18

Guard _____ *'s life and rescue her; let her never be put to shame. May integrity and uprightness protect her, and cause her to put her hope fully in you.*   PSALM 25:20–21

Help _____ *to stand firm, with the belt of truth buckled securely around his waist and the breastplate of righteousness guarding his heart.*   EPHESIANS 6:14

Cause _____ *to be careful to lead a blameless life, having nothing to do with evil. Do not let her slander her friends or classmates in secret, and keep her from practicing deceit or speaking falsely. Keep your eyes on her and draw her near to you, so that she might stand in your presence.*

PSALM 101:2–7

Satan is a liar and the father of lies. Don't allow _____ *to listen to Satan or carry out his desires; rather, cause him to tune his ear to hear what you say. Let him receive and believe the truth that you speak, knowing that you are his Father and that he belongs to you.*   JOHN 8:42–47

Let _____ always be a truthful witness, no matter whether she is defending her faith or giving a report about something that she has seen or done. Show her how much you detest lying lips, and cause her to see the extravagant delight that you take in her when she is truthful.

PROVERBS 12:17, 22

Keep _____ from willful sins. May the words of his mouth and the meditations of his heart be pleasing in your sight.

PSALM 19:13 – 14

Cause _____ to hold to your teaching, to be your disciple, and to know the truth — and let your truth set her free.

JOHN 8:31 – 32

CHAPTER 2

Praying for an Others-Centered Outlook

Do nothing out of selfish ambition or vain conceit,
but in humility consider others better than yourselves.
Each of you should look not only to your own interests,
but also to the interests of others.

PHILIPPIANS 2:3 – 4

"The world does not revolve around you."

How many times have you said — or at least thought — those words as you looked at your teen? In a brief, informal survey of some of my friends regarding teens and self-centeredness, here's a snippet of what I heard: "My daughter definitely thinks she's 'all that.'" "Right now, my son is the center of his universe." "I just wish she would wake up and realize that there are other people living in our house."

Self-centeredness is, of course, a human condition — teens aren't the only ones who suffer from it. But as editors Joe White and Jim Weidmann point out in their book *The Spiritual Mentoring of Teens*, the teen years tend to bring out an "acuteness of self" in kids. They say that "if self-centeredness were a disease, most teens would be diagnosed with at least a mild case, and many would be classified as suffering from 'chronic, inflamed egotism.'"[1]

---

1. Joe White and Jim Weidmann, ed., *The Spiritual Mentoring of Teens* (Wheaton, Ill.: Tyndale House, 2001), 401.

White is the director of Kanakuk Kamps and, for what it's worth, he is the most inspirational and encouraging speaker I have ever heard when it comes to parenting teens. One of the main goals of the Kanakuk program is to teach kids to put God first, others second, and themselves third. This "I'm Third" principle is based on Jesus' teaching in Matthew 22:36–40, where he tells a Pharisee that the greatest commandment is to love God "with all your heart and with all your soul and with all your mind," and that the second greatest commandment is to "love your neighbor as yourself." Our kids have all attended Kanakuk, and every time I see the "I'm Third" sign on Hillary's bedroom mirror, I thank God for the camp staff and counselors who so beautifully model this way of life for some 17,000 campers every summer.

If we want to help our teens develop a heart for service, sometimes one of the best things we can do is to get them out of their comfort zones and encourage them to look beyond their high school lives to see the bigger world "out there." Our church routinely sends groups of young people on short-term missions to poorer areas of the United States, as well as to such far-flung locations as Tanzania, Thailand, the Dominican Republic, and China. For some parents, like my friend Michelle, sending a teen to the other side of the world demands mountains of prayer, lots of deep breaths, and an entire suitcase full of things like Band-Aids and hand sanitizer. But even with all of her maternal worries and concerns, Michelle would be the first to tell you that, for her daughter Julia, going to China was truly an answer to prayer ...

"Open yours next, Julia!"

Six-year-old Amanda's voice cut across the dining room. She idolized her older sister, and as the family gathered to celebrate the New Year on January 1, she was eager to see what was on Julia's scrap of paper. Twelve months earlier, each family member had written a list of goals for the coming year. Now, clustered as they were around the dining room table, the time had come to revisit these objectives to see what the year—and God—had brought.

Michelle gazed at her fourteen-year-old daughter with a bittersweet mixture of concern, pride, and joy. Her mind wandered back to the previous year, when Julia was in the eighth grade. It had been a tough season for them both. As a student at a small, private school, Julia did not have a large peer group, and she had wrestled with loneliness. On weekends, she had often stayed home while her high school-aged sister, Chelsea, darted from one friend's house or party to the next. For Michelle's part, the difficulty had come in learning to trust God to bring something good out of that painful time. Looking across the table, she realized that God had, indeed, shown himself faithful. If nothing else, the time that Julia had spent alone had served to deepen her relationship with God and heighten her sensitivity to the emotional needs of others.

It had started, Michelle thought, in China. Julia had gone on a three-week summer mission trip, where she helped run an English language camp for children. In the months leading up to the trip, Michelle had prayed several very specific prayers. In addition to asking God to protect the team, she prayed that Julia would be a blessing to others, that she would find a special friend in China, and—knowing that the language barrier could pose a problem—that the spiritual language of God's love would flow through Julia and the other missionaries and into the hearts of the Chinese children.

Unable to communicate with her daughter—or anyone else on the trip, for that matter—for three long weeks left Michelle hungry for information. When the group finally returned, she couldn't wait to hear all the details—and she was not disappointed. Julia stayed up almost all night long, tears streaming down her face, recounting story after story of the Chinese people and her newfound love for them. One girl, in particular, had captured Julia's heart. Despite her own obvious material needs, little "Abby" had insisted on giving Julia her favorite bracelet as a token of their friendship.

"It was definitely a culture shock," Julia acknowledged. "Being in China made me so aware of the extremes of life—the big difference between the lives of the rich and the poor. The Chinese children had so little, but they gave so much. It was just amazing."

Abby—who, like the other Chinese children, had chosen an English name that the mission team could remember and pronounce—represented the answer to Michelle's prayer for Julia to find a friend. But there was more. Suddenly, Julia's desire for friends and activity-filled weekends didn't matter as much as it had before. Working with Abby and the other Chinese children had opened Julia's eyes to the joy that comes through serving others, and she decided to look for a place where she could minister in a similar way closer to home.

She didn't have to look far. Her church was sponsoring a back-to-school party for a group of needy children in the community, and Julia jumped in, raising more than $800 to help fill backpacks with school supplies. Later, when she learned that the kids and their families had very little warm clothing for the winter, she organized a drive to supply them with blankets, clothing, and shoes. She called it "Blanket the Neighborhood." Watching her efforts, one neighbor finally wondered why Julia seemed so different from most teenage girls — the ones who spent their time thinking about their appearance and their social standing.

"Oh, I worry about those things, too," Julia had assured her. "I fuss over my hair and makeup and stuff. But, you know, when you're busy filling forty-two backpacks or playing games with the kids, you don't have much time to think about those things."

Remembering those words, Michelle had to smile. Julia, she knew, spent *plenty* of time on her hair. But her primary delight still came from helping others — like Lainey, the young girl Julia had met while handing out blankets. When she learned that there was a mentoring program in Lainey's neighborhood, Julia immediately decided that she wanted to be Lainey's "Big Sister." The two girls had become fast friends — and now, on New Year's Day, Lainey was definitely part of their family.

"Yeah, Julia, open your paper!" Lainey urged, joining Amanda's cries and drawing Michelle's attention back to the party. "We want to see what you wrote!"

Slowly, Julia unfolded the paper. It seemed hard to believe that a whole year had passed since she had last seen her goals. "I want to become more self-confident," she read aloud.

That one, Michelle noted, had definitely happened. Whether Julia realized it or not, her decision to focus on others instead of herself had given her a sense of purpose and a peace that had not always been there.

"I want to do a good cause."

"Well, you blanketed the neighborhood," Chelsea pointed out. "You can check that one off."

Julia's next resolution drew a round of laughter: "I want to walk the dog." And then came one that pierced Michelle's heart: "I want to get more friends."

That particular goal, Michelle knew, mirrored her own prayers for Julia—and God had come through. Julia had started her ninth grade year at a new school, and almost without realizing it, she found herself settling into a new group of friends, with a social calendar that was definitely picking up steam.

"Are there any more things on your list?" Lainey asked.

"Just one," Julia answered. "I said that I want to change someone's life."

For a moment, nobody spoke. And then Lainey looked over at the piece of paper and read Julia's words for herself. She looked up, her big brown eyes speaking words that she could not express.

"You've changed *my* life," she said softly.

Just as God, Michelle realized, had changed Julia's.

Prayer Principle

A short-term mission trip or service in a local shelter
can take a teen out of her comfort zone and open
her eyes to the joy that comes with putting the
needs of others ahead of her own.

Poised for Prayer

I love Michelle's family tradition of writing down goals, or prayer requests, every year, and then ushering in the New Year by looking to see what God has done. I also love the fact that Michelle prays for her four children every day, logging many of her requests in a prayer journal that she has kept for as long as I have known her. When I interviewed her for this chapter, she was able to look back over the years and see a track record of God's faithfulness — tangible evidence that he had heard, and answered, the deepest cries of her heart.

Michelle has four kids. They are all girls, but — as is the case with pretty much every family — they have very different needs. Knowing that she has years of experience as a praying parent, I asked Michelle if she had any favorite prayers.

"I love to pray that my daughters would have the fruit of the Holy Spirit manifested in their lives," she told me. "When I open my prayer journal in the morning, I ask God to show me if there is any aspect of the Holy Spirit's fruit that one or another of my girls might need in extra measure that day."

She was talking about the fruit listed in Galatians 5:22: Love, joy, peace, patience, kindness, goodness, faithfulness, gentleness, and self-control. When Julia was in China, Michelle asked God to let these qualities flow through her every day. The fact that Julia came home from that trip with such an others-centered outlook doesn't surprise me; the fruit that Michelle prayed for is the very thing that our kids need if they are to, as Galatians 5:13 puts it, "serve one another in love."

Whether you are praying for an end to the "me, myself, and I" attitude, or whether your prayers are for something else entirely, I want to encourage you to follow Michelle's example and, if you are not already doing so, start keeping a prayer journal. You can pour out your heart over three or four pages, or just grab a Scripture or two from the list below and write it out, complete with your teen's name and today's date, bullet-point style. Try it for a month. You will build an impressive collection of requests—and you will begin to see the fingerprints of God's provision. Try it for a year, and you'll be amazed. Things you forgot that you even cared or prayed about will be there, in black and white, for you to see—and for you to marvel at God's goodness. Armed with the evidence, you'll be equipped to follow the charge Paul outlines in Philippians 4:6: "Tell God your needs and don't forget to thank him for his answers" (LB).

As you pray, let your teen know what you are doing. Even if he doesn't put much stock in prayer now, the mental image of you praying—the knowledge that you are bringing his needs before the throne of Almighty God—is something that he will carry with him forever. It will help set the stage for his own prayer life as he learns to look beyond his own interests and bring the needs of his friends, his family, and his coworkers to the Lord. And when the answers come, rather than focusing on himself, your teen will be ready to "tell the next generation the praiseworthy deeds of the LORD, his power, and the wonders he has done."[1]

---

1. Psalm 78:4.

Prayers You Can Use

Heavenly Father,

Fill _____ with your Holy Spirit, and let the Spirit's fruit be evident in his life. Let his words, his thoughts, and his actions be marked by love, joy, peace, patience, kindness, goodness, faithfulness, gentleness, and self-control.

GALATIANS 5:22

Let _____ put you first, others second, and herself third as she follows your commandments. May she love you with all of her heart, soul, and mind, and let her love others as much as she loves herself.   MATTHEW 22:37 – 39

Turn _____'s heart toward your statutes and not toward selfish gain.   PSALM 119:36

Cause _____ to become great in your sight. Let him be a leader who serves, someone whose idea of being "first" is to become a slave to others. Show him how to follow the example of Jesus, who came not to be served, but to serve.

MATTHEW 20:26 – 28

Let _____ do nothing out of selfish ambition or vain conceit, but cause her, in humility, to consider others—her family, her friends, her classmates—as better than herself. Cause her to look beyond her own interests to focus on the interests and needs of other people.   PHILIPPIANS 2:3–4

Teach _____ to be kind to the needy, for in so doing, he will honor you.   PROVERBS 14:31

I pray that _____ would be wise and understanding—and that the evidence of these traits would be seen in her good deeds, done in humility. Do not let her harbor bitter envy or selfish ambition in her heart, because those things come from the devil and lead to disorder and every evil practice.

JAMES 3:13–16

Let _____ realize that if he has everything except love, then he is nothing. Cause his life to be marked by your love, Lord—the kind that is patient and kind, and never envious, boastful, proud, rude, or self-seeking.

1 CORINTHIANS 13: 2–5

Remind _____ that when she reaches out with food, clothing, hospitality, and other evidences of your love, whatever she does for "the least of these brothers and sisters" she is doing for you.   MATTHEW 25:34–40

When _____ claims to have faith in you, impress on his heart the need to accompany his words and beliefs with actions—the kind of good deeds and selfless actions that prove that his faith is real.   JAMES 2:14–17

Equip and embolden _____ to defend the cause of the weak and fatherless and to protect the rights of the poor and the oppressed. Open her ears so that she can hear and respond to the cries of a world in need.   PSALM 82:3; PROVERBS 21:13

I pray that in whatever _____ does, he would seek to bring glory to you rather than to himself. Let him never seek his own good but the good of many, as he follows the example of Christ.   1 CORINTHIANS 10:31 – 11:1

Make _____ rich in every way so that she can be generous on every occasion, so that people will give thanks to you.   2 CORINTHIANS 9:11

CHAPTER 3

Praying for a Humble, Teachable Heart

Remind the people to be subject to rulers and authorities,
to be obedient, to be ready to do whatever is good,
to slander no one, to be peaceable and considerate,
and to show true humility toward all men.

TITUS 3:1–2

"Life's not fair."

If this isn't one of the most trotted-out lines in the history of parenting, then I don't know what is. I've used it on my kids when refs make questionable calls, when teachers impose extra-tough grading standards, and when my husband and I say no to something that our teens don't agree with or understand.

I'll never forget the day our son, Robbie, came home from basketball practice with his nose out of joint. His coach had awarded a prize to one of the players for making the most free throws — and Robbie was convinced that he'd seen the fellow step over the line. "It's not fair!" Robbie said. "He cheated!"

"Life's not fair," I countered. "Especially in sports. There are going to be ball hogs among your teammates, bad calls from the refs, and coaching decisions that you don't understand or agree with. How you respond to these things says a lot about who you are as a player—and as a person."

"Well, it's not right," Robbie muttered, before heading off to do his homework.

Later that night, the subject came up again. "Mom," Robbie said, "I keep going over that shot in my mind. I asked God to help me realize that Austin didn't cheat—but every time I remember the shot, I think that he did!"

"Maybe he did," I sighed. "But maybe that's not the point. Maybe God is giving you this opportunity to give up your right to be right. Maybe he wants you to learn to honor your coach and humbly accept his decision—even though that's not the way *you* would have done it."

I was on a roll. "You know," I continued, "the Bible says that God's ways are not our ways.[1] What if we questioned God every time he did something that we didn't understand or agree with?"

"But God is God! Of *course* he does stuff that we don't understand!"

"I know!" I laughed. "But I think that he uses people like coaches—or parents or teachers or bosses—to help us practice accepting the things we may not understand. He wants us to be humble and teachable instead of being stubborn or proud or wanting to quit or argue when things don't go the way we think they should. If you can learn to honor your coaches and your teachers—even if you don't always agree with them—then you will be able to respect God and obey him, even when you don't understand or agree with one of his commands."

---

1. Isaiah 55:8.

I thought it was one of my better parenting speeches. I could see the wheels turning in Robbie's mind, and I hoped he could follow my logic—but I worried that what he was really doing was replaying Austin's shot for the umpteenth time in his head, searching for a way to make sense out of the coach's decision. "Do you see what I mean?" I finally asked.

"I guess so," Robbie said slowly.

And that, I realized, was as good as it was going to get.

A few months later, I remembered my conversation with Robbie when I got a phone call from a girlfriend who had just returned from a round of college recruiting visits with her soccer-phenom of a daughter.

"The coach at one school told me that they aren't just looking at the players' stats—how many assists they have, how many goals they score, or how many state championships their teams have won," my friend said. "When they send scouts to a game, they don't just watch the players *on* the field; they watch to see how a girl reacts when she is pulled *off* the field. Does she sulk? Sit at the end of the bench? Roll her eyes? Ignore the coaches? Get on her cell phone? Does she—"

"Do players *really* get on their cell phones during a game?" I interrupted.

"Oh, you'd be surprised. But that's not the point. The point is that the college scouts are looking for players who are open to correction and who are willing to interact with their coaches to see how they can make changes and improve their play.

"And you know what?" my friend continued. "I think that's how God looks at us. He is always watching us to see how we respond to correction and how we react when things don't go our way."

Wow. Maybe Robbie hadn't totally connected the dots between his relationship to his coach and his relationship to God, but my girlfriend had, and that was all the inspiration I needed to redouble my prayer efforts for my kids to have humble, teachable hearts—whether they were on the athletic field, in the classroom, or just sitting around our dinner table.

I know that God hears prayers like these. A couple of years after *Praying the Scriptures for Your Children* was released, a mom at church pulled me aside and told me what God had done in her son's life ...

"I'm having some problems with Ryan."

Melanie knew that the teacher on the other end of the telephone was serious, but she was the PE teacher, for goodness sake. How bad could the problems be?

"He's trying to run the class," the woman explained.

"Oh." Melanie didn't know what to say. "I'll talk to him about it," she offered.

"Thanks," the teacher said. "Ryan is a very talented young man—and he is extremely competitive. I love the fact that he always gives it everything he has, but the trouble is that he doesn't take correction very well."

Melanie knew exactly what the teacher meant. Ryan was a strong athlete, and as such, he had been able to get away with some sloppy habits. But as other players honed their skills, they were sure to catch up with him—and if the lack of finesse didn't sideline him one day, Melanie worried that Ryan's stubborn attitude would.

She picked up her copy of *Praying the Scriptures for Your Children* and flipped to the back of the chapter that targeted kids' relationships with teachers and coaches. "Cause _____ to obey his teachers and coaches and submit to their authority," she read. "Let him know that these people keep watch over him and that you will hold them accountable for the job they do. Show _____ that when he obeys his teachers and coaches and makes their work a joy instead of a burden, the end result will be to his advantage. (Hebrews 13:17)."[1]

That was exactly the sort of prayer that Melanie wanted. She mentally inserted Ryan's name into the blanks, and then called her son into the room.

"Ryan," she said, "I want to show you something." Melanie opened her Bible to the book of Hebrews, and showed her son the verse that she had prayed. "God wants you to listen to your PE teacher. The teacher knows what she wants you to do, and you need to do it. God says that when you make her job a joy instead of a burden, it will wind up being a good thing for you in the end."

Ryan knew that his mother meant business. She was giving him an opportunity to respond to his teacher's correction — and to her own prayers. He could take it or leave it. He decided to take it.

It wasn't long before Melanie happened to see the PE teacher at school. "Hey!" the teacher said, "You won't believe what's happened. Ryan's attitude has totally turned around — it's like a miracle!"

Melanie was thrilled — but found herself back on her knees a couple of years later when Ryan's younger brothers grew up

---

1. Jodie Berndt, *Praying the Scriptures for Your Children* (Grand Rapids: Zondervan, 2001), 185.

and found themselves in the same teacher's class. Like their older brother, the boys made no secret of their impatience with the woman's coaching methods. Couldn't she see that they knew how the games ought to be played?

Melanie knew that the same God who had worked such a change in Ryan's life could do the same thing for her other boys. "Lord," she prayed, "cause Wilson and Spencer to obey their teacher and submit to her authority ..." She finished praying Hebrews 13:17 again and continued to ask God to work in her younger sons' lives as they grew.

Melanie had a sense that God was answering her prayers—at the very least, she wasn't getting any phone calls from frustrated teachers—but nothing could have prepared her for the surprise that lay in store. At the graduation ceremony, two students were honored for the "Most Improved Sportsmanship" award: Wilson and Spencer! Thinking of the last few words in Hebrews 13:17—that when our kids obey their leaders and submit to their authority, the end result will be to their advantage—Melanie couldn't help but marvel at the goodness of God.

Prayer Principle

When you pray for your teen
to humbly submit to authority,
you are setting him up to reap God's rewards.

Poised for Prayer

The Bible is brimming with examples of folks who were willing to submit to God and learn from him; Moses, for instance, was known as "a very humble man, more humble than anyone else on the face of the earth."[1] There are also plenty of examples of what can happen when humans exalt themselves and refuse to acknowledge God's authority—folks like King Nebuchadnezzar, who spent seven years eating grass and living like a wild animal because of his own arrogance and pride.[2]

On the humble roster, I find myself drawn to John the Baptist. As a young locust-eater, John was no stranger to recognition—crowds jostled to get near him, and he had a posse of disciples who were bigger fans than any clique of high school cheerleaders. But when the curiosity seekers and autograph hounds demanded to know who he was and tried to get him to talk about himself, he never took the bait. Instead, he continually talked about Jesus, saying that he was coming—and that he was someone whose sandals he, John, was not worthy even to untie.

Ultimately, when Jesus showed up, John was the first to recognize him. Had I been John, I think I would have told all of my friends that "I saw him first!" My story would have gotten better with each telling, until my accomplishment—spotting the Lord—threatened to eclipse Christ's very appearance. But not John. John admitted that he recognized Jesus when he saw the Holy Spirit descend on him in the form of a dove—but he quickly pointed out that he would never have known what it all meant, had God not clued him in as to what to look for![3]

---

1. Numbers 12:3.   2. See Daniel 4:28–37.   3. John 1:19–34.

I love John's humility. Had he been an athlete, I bet he would have had the all-time record for assists, only we'd never know it because he would get us to spend so much time looking at Jesus — the leading scorer — that we'd forget all about his accomplishments. Had he been a musician, I bet that he would have been willing to play second fiddle, providing the harmony to complement — and never overpower — the guy who sat in the first chair. Had he been an actor, I bet he would have made sure to turn the spotlight, and the loudest applause, on the one who directed the play.

Proverbs 18:12 (NLT) reads, "Haughtiness goes before destruction; humility precedes honor." When I pray for my teens, I pray that they will be like John the Baptist — a man who had plenty to be proud of, but who chose humility instead. I pray that they will never seek glory or attention for themselves but that they will give credit to others. Most of all, I pray that they will show respect for their teachers, coaches, and peers — whether they are serving on the student council or sitting in the back row of a math class — so their character and their conduct will bring honor to Jesus Christ.

Prayers like these take faith. To resist authority and seek honor and attention for yourself is human nature — and believe me, our family is *plenty* human. But as I pray for my teens — and as you pray for yours — we can do so knowing that we serve a God who delights in those who honor him and who is able to do immeasurably more in our kids' lives than all we ask or imagine.[1]

---

1. Psalm 147:11 NLT; Ephesians 3:20.

Prayers You Can Use

Heavenly Father,

Remind _____ to be subject to the rulers and authorities in his life, to be obedient, and to slander no one — even if he does not agree with decisions that his teachers or coaches make. Prompt him to be considerate and to show true humility toward everyone. TITUS 3:1 – 2

Let _____ give you the praise and glory for the talents and abilities you have given her. Remind her that everything she has comes from you alone. 1 CHRONICLES 29:11 – 14

Cause _____ to be submissive and respectful toward those who are older and more experienced than he is. Let him be clothed with humility, remembering that you oppose the proud but give grace to the humble, and that you will lift him up in due time. 1 PETER 5:5 – 6

Show _____ what you require: that she act justly, love mercy, and walk humbly with you, dear God. Teach her that these attributes matter more to you than any worldly success or accomplishments. MICAH 6:8

Help _____ to do nothing out of selfish ambition or vain conceit. Cause him to respond to his coaches and team-mates with humility, considering them better than himself. Don't allow him to think only of his own needs or interests, but help him to be a team player, focusing on giving others support and credit.   PHILIPPIANS 2:3–4

Let _____ be honest in her estimate of her abilities, measuring her value not by worldly success but by the faith that you have given her. Open her eyes so that she can see the different gifts and talents that you have given to others.

ROMANS 12:3–6

Remind _____ that pride goes before destruction and a haughty spirit before a fall. As he responds to his teachers and coaches, let him pay close attention to their instruction, so that he will prosper.   PROVERBS 16:18–20

Help _____ to obey her leaders and submit to their authority. Remind her that they will be held accountable for the teaching and training they are giving her, and that if she honors them, it will benefit her in the end.   HEBREWS 13:17

Cause _____ to be wise in the way that he acts toward coaches, referees, teammates, and opponents. Let him make the most of every opportunity, using words that are gracious and effective, so that nothing he says or does will bring dishonor to your name. COLOSSIANS 4:5–6

Prompt _____ to acknowledge that you are sovereign over the kingdoms on earth, and that the authorities in her life have been put there by you. DANIEL 5:21

Teach _____ to listen to advice and accept instruction so that, in the end, he will be wise. PROVERBS 19:20

As you do immeasurably more than all we could ever ask or imagine in _____'s life, let our entire family remember to give you the glory, for ever and ever! Amen.

EPHESIANS 3:20–21

CHAPTER 4

Praying through Anger to Composure

Better to be patient than powerful;
better to have self-control than to conquer a city.
PROVERBS 16:32 NLT

"Is it a sin to get angry?"

I posed the question to our four children as we sat around the dinner table one night. I wasn't sure how they'd respond and — in an effort to keep them from influencing one another's opinions — I called for a quick "up or down" vote, no talking allowed.

Is it a sin to get angry?

Two kids said yes; two said no.

My question stemmed from a conversation I'd had with a high school counselor. Over the years, he has worked with countless teens and their families — people representing an incredibly wide range of spiritual beliefs and convictions. As we discussed anger, he told me that in some of the Christian families he has counseled, kids are so afraid to express their anger — fearing that it is a sin and something that has no place in a Christian's life — that they bottle it up until they can't hold it any longer and it comes out in destructive ways: things like bad attitudes, unkind or negative remarks, and violence.

I cringed when I heard that, wondering about my own kids; and when 50 percent of them flunked my pop quiz, I hurried to do a little damage control. "Anger is not a sin," I told them. "The Bible says that we aren't supposed to be easily angered or quick-tempered, and that when someone—or something— makes us mad, we can't let the situation go unresolved. But all of us have times when we get mad; that's just part of life."

As is often the case when I think I'm teaching the kids an important lesson, they didn't seem to be all that impressed by my insights. "OK," one of them said, "anger isn't a sin. Can I have the last roll?"

Anger may not be a sin, but that doesn't mean that it isn't a tricky subject. And when it comes to dealing with anger—or more to the point, when it comes to helping our teens deal with their anger—the problem can be complicated by the fact that we may not know what is making them mad. Sometimes they don't either! It could be an argument with a friend or a rejection (real or imagined) by one of their peers. It could be a hurt that hasn't healed—maybe from a divorce that happened five years ago or from harsh words that were spoken yesterday. It could be the result of unmet expectations or of some sort of anxiety, such as worrying that they'll fail a test or get cut from a team.

Prayer Principle

When our teen is angry,
we may not understand why.
But that's OK, because God does.

Sometimes we will be able to discover what lies behind our teen's anger; sometimes we won't. The good news is that God knows. He "searches every heart and understands every motive behind the thoughts."[1] He knows what makes our kids tick—and what ticks them off—and when we bring our concerns before his throne, he will show us exactly how we should pray . . .

Sandy hung up the phone and turned to her husband, Jay, torn between anger and shame. Had their son really been arrested?

"How could he do such a thing?" Sandy cried.

Andrew, who was away at college, had evidently gotten into an argument with his girlfriend. The exchange had grown heated, and—in a fit of rage—he had pushed her, causing her to fall. Onlookers had called the police.

"I just can't believe it," Sandy said. "I mean, he's never done *anything* like this before."

Jay understood Sandy's frustration, but like her, he had no answers. Years ago, when Andrew was still in middle school, they had taken him to a counselor, who had assured them that their son's occasional negativity and tendency toward sarcasm were fairly normal traits in adolescent boys. They had been reassured, but they continued to pray for Andrew's character development as he grew.

College had ushered in a new host of concerns, not the least of which was the alcohol that seemed to pervade almost every aspect of campus life. Andrew didn't always make the best choices, but he had never been violent. Theirs was a fam-

---

1. 1 Chronicles 28:9.

ily marked by mutual respect, and Andrew and his younger siblings had all the love they could ever want — not to mention every other physical and spiritual advantage. Sandy was certain that, in their home, at least, Andrew had never, ever, been exposed to any sort of physical abuse. Why, she and Jay hardly ever even raised their voices!

In the days that followed Andrew's arrest, Sandy's emotions ran the gamut from anger (she was horrified by her son's actions) to shame (how could he have come from their family?) to despair. Sandy pored over the pages in her Bible, desperate to know how God could ever use such an ugly, painful incident for good.

One of her favorite prayers came from 2 Corinthians 10:3–5, a passage that she had been praying over Andrew for about seven years. "Lord," she prayed again, "demolish the strongholds in Andrew's life. Demolish arguments and every pretension that sets itself up against the knowledge of you. Take all of Andrew's thoughts and make them obedient to Christ."

Sandy thought about the strongholds that she had prayed against over the years — those mental, emotional, and spiritual fortresses that had seemed from time to time to capture Andrew's mind. She had prayed about pride, rebellion, depression, fear, and even materialism. She had asked God to protect her son and to keep his heart and mind free from Satan's lies. God had answered those prayers, she knew, but something was missing.

Two days later, Sandy was driving to church, crying out to God and asking him — for what seemed like the millionth time — to please do *something* in Andrew's life. Suddenly, almost as clearly as if he were sitting in the seat next to her, she heard God's voice. "Sandy," the Lord said, "all these years you have been praying for the strongholds to come down in Andrew's life. Now, you know how to name the stronghold. It is anger. Pray—and *watch me pull it down*."

There it was—the ray of hope that Sandy needed. She began to pray with a renewed fervor, specifically asking God to tear down the fortress of anger that held Andrew captive. And slowly but surely he did.

It has been more than a year since Sandy began praying specifically about Andrew's anger. During that time, she and Jay have watched their son confront his past mistakes, both via a court-ordered anger management program as well as through a good dose of self-introspection. He has experienced genuine remorse, repenting of both attitudes and actions. The transformation has been so amazing that Sandy and Jay asked Andrew to undergo some psychological testing, just to be certain that no other problems were hidden under their son's newfound peace and humility.

"Andrew is still a work in progress," Sandy told me, "but I am totally blown away by all that the Lord has done in his heart and in his life. Jay and I still don't really understand the source of Andrew's anger. It is mysterious to us—but not to God. And I believe that as Andrew continues to grow in the Lord, our understanding—and his healing—will continue. We are amazed at the difference we see in our son every single day.

"And more importantly," she concluded, "so is he."

Poised for Prayer

Anger, as my kids will now tell you, is not a sin. Nor is it something that will prevent our teen from being used by God—just look at the apostle Peter! When Jesus met Peter, his very first words were, "Come, follow me." He repeated that command during their last recorded conversation, saying "You must follow me!"[1] In between these bookends—and for the rest of Peter's earthly life—he did exactly that. He was a guy who cursed and swore, who thought he could rebuke the Lord, and who whipped out his sword and sliced off a soldier's ear when the Pharisees came to arrest Jesus.[2] He was hardly a model citizen—and yet, with all of his failings, Peter managed to stumble and leap and sink and grab his way toward Jesus. He didn't dwell on his outbursts or his flaws; he simply followed Jesus.

We can teach our teens to do the same thing. Scripture outlines a beautiful and effective prescription for dealing with anger. Consider how Ephesians 4:26–27 reads in the following three translations:

- New International Version: " 'In your anger do not sin': Do not let the sun go down while you are still angry, and do not give the devil a foothold."
- New Living Translation: "And 'don't sin by letting anger gain control over you.' Don't let the sun go down while you are still angry, for anger gives a mighty foothold to the Devil."
- New American Standard Bible: " 'Be angry, and yet do not sin'; do not let the sun go down on your anger, and do not give the devil an opportunity."

---

1. See Matthew 4:19; John 21:19.   2. See Matthew 16:22; 26:74; John 18:11.

I like those plainspoken words: *Be angry, and yet do not sin.* Anger, in other words, is not the problem. The problem is sin—the sin that can happen when our kids allow anger to have free rein over their thoughts and actions. Left unattended, anger can burn out of control, consuming friendships and destroying both tangible and intangible things of value. Even more frightening, it gives Satan the chance he wants—the chance he *craves*—to rip jagged and painful holes in our kids' lives.

Throughout the Bible, the pattern is clear: If we are angry with someone, our job is not to get even or to nurse a grudge or even to simply ignore the problem. Our job is to try and make things right. As we pray for our teens in this critical area, let's point them toward the solution outlined in Romans 12:17–21. These verses come at the tail end of an entire passage that details how Christians are supposed to live transformed lives—lives marked by things such as humility, service, generosity, and love.

In a nutshell, here's how Romans 12 can equip us to pray for our kids:

- that they would behave honorably, never repaying evil with evil, but taking care to do the right thing;
- that they would do everything in their power to live at peace with others, knowing that when they do their part, the results are up to God;
- that they would never try to take revenge, but that they would let God—whose wrath always includes his mercy—be the one to repay those who deserve it;

- that they would channel their anger into blessings, looking for ways to provide good things for those who have wronged them, that their enemies might be ashamed of their past actions; and
- that they would never be controlled by anger or let evil get the best of them, but that they would be empowered by the Holy Spirit to overcome evil with good.

The Bible is full of passages such as these, as well as stories and illustrations that underscore the value of things such as praying for our enemies and living at peace with others. It also has plenty of stories about folks who got angry and lost their cool, just as Peter did.

As we pray for our teens, then, let's keep the picture of Peter in mind. He might have been rash and hot-tempered, but he got it right in the end, urging other Christians to be self-controlled, to show respect to others, to bear up under the pain of unjust suffering, and—I love this one—to never "repay evil with evil or insult with insult, but with blessing."[1]

This, Peter says, is the kind of life to which our teens are called. All it takes is a willingness to do just what Peter did: follow Jesus—and when they stumble or fall, to get up and follow again.[2]

---

1. 1 Peter 1:13; 2:17, 19–20; 3:9.   2. 1 Peter 2:21.

Prayers You Can Use

Heavenly Father,

Teach _____ how to be just like you: compassionate and gracious, slow to anger, abounding in love and faithfulness. PSALM 86:15

Don't let _____ be like a fool who gives full vent to his anger, but cause him to be wise and to keep himself under control. PROVERBS 29:11

When _____ gets angry with someone or something, please guard her heart to keep her from sinning. Do not let her anger smolder or last, and do not allow it to control her. Keep Satan and his schemes far from _____, so that he will not be able to attack her in this vulnerable area.

EPHESIANS 4:26–32

Cause _____ to be quick to listen, slow to speak, and slow to become angry, and remind him that a person's anger does not bring about the righteous life that you desire.

JAMES 1:19–20

Let _____'s life be marked by love—the kind that is not easily angered and that keeps no record of wrongs.

1 CORINTHIANS 13:5

*Show _____ that when she lashes out in anger, calling
someone an idiot or a fool, she puts herself in danger. Let her
be quick to reach out and be reconciled with anyone who has
anything against her, so that she can be free to enjoy sweet
fellowship with you.* MATTHEW 5:23–24

*Do not allow _____ to repay evil with evil or insult
with insult, but show him how to respond to these offenses
with blessings, that he might receive the reward and the inheritance that you have for him.* 1 PETER 3:9

*Demolish the stronghold of anger in _____'s life. Do
not let Satan build a fortress of lies in her mind; rather, take
all of her thoughts and make them obedient to Christ.*

2 CORINTHIANS 10:4–5

*Help _____ to get rid of all anger, rage, malice, slan-
der, and filthy language in his life, clothing himself instead
with things like compassion, kindness, humility, gentleness,
patience, and love. Cause _____ to bear with the
faults of others even those who anger or offend him, and to
be quick to forgive. Let the peace of Christ rule in his heart.*

COLOSSIANS 3:8–15

Equip _____ to live by the Spirit, so that she will not live to gratify the desires of this sinful nature. Fill her with the Holy Spirit's fruit, that her life might be marked by things like peace, gentleness, and self-control.

GALATIANS 5:19–22

Guard _____'s heart so that he will not want to take revenge. Let him be content to leave room for your wrath, knowing that you have vowed to avenge and repay—and that you will take care of every situation in your perfect timing.   DEUTERONOMY 32:35

Give _____ strength, and bless her with peace.

PSALM 29:11

May grace and peace be _____'s in abundance through the knowledge of God and of Jesus our Lord.   2 PETER 1:2

CHAPTER 5

Praying for Compassion and Kindness

Make every effort to add to your faith goodness;
and to goodness ... brotherly kindness;
and to brotherly kindness, love.
For if you possess these qualities in increasing measure,
they will keep you from being ineffective and unproductive
in your knowledge of our Lord Jesus Christ.

2 PETER 1:5, 7–8

When I began working on this book, I contacted some friends who work at the Moms in Prayer (formerly Moms In Touch) International headquarters in Poway, California.[1] I knew that they were well acquainted with the idea of using Bible verses to help shape their prayers, and I figured that, stationed as they are in the epicenter of an international network of praying moms, they would have plenty of stories to share. Sure enough, within a week, my email box was loaded with their replies.

If you are a parent who bought this book because you wanted to know how to pray about things like "sex, drugs, and rock 'n' roll," I want to assure you that I'm right there with you. Our teens need those "crisis control" kinds of prayers. But they also need our prayers for everyday challenges — things

---

1. For more information on Moms in Prayer, please visit the website at www.momsinprayer.org. See the appendix in this book for contact information.

like humility in victory, perseverance in difficulty, and kindness in the face of opportunity.

Sprinkled among the stories in my in-box was this little gem from a mother named Marlae, who serves as the executive vice president of Moms in Prayer. Hers is not the kind of answered prayer that would make the evening news report; rather, it stands as a testimony to the power and importance of talking to God about the things that could slip by unnoticed in the blur that is teenage life. As you read Marlae's story, I hope you'll find it as encouraging as I did.

Marlae picked up the phone and cocked her head, nestling the receiver between her shoulder and her ear as she opened the refrigerator. "Hello?" she said, placing a gallon of milk and a tub of sour cream on one of the shelves.

"Hi, Marlae," came a voice she did not recognize. "You might not remember me, but my daughter Ashley is in Joshua's class at school. You'll probably think I'm crazy for calling, but I just had to tell you what Ashley said about your son."

Marlae's hand paused as she pulled a bunch of carrots out of the grocery bag. She wondered what the caller would say.

"Ashley said that Joshua is one of the kindest guys she knows at school. He takes time to say hello to all of the kids in the hallways — not just the ones who are popular. I just thought you'd want to know."

Marlae wanted to laugh out loud. Not two days earlier she had prayed for her seventeen-year-old son, using words from Ephesians 4:32: "May Joshua be kind and compassionate to others, forgiving others just as you forgave us in Christ, O

Lord." At six foot three, Joshua didn't *look* like a meek or compassionate soul, but that didn't stop Marlae from asking God to fill her son with these attributes.

As she thanked the caller and hung up the phone, Marlae's mind wandered back four years to a time when Joshua was not quite so tall—or so confident. Like most thirteen-year-old boys, Josh was a little unsure of himself, particularly when it came to girls. One of Marlae's chief concerns was that he would not allow the pressure to be "cool" to keep him from being a good friend to his classmates. Marlae wanted him to be kind and compassionate to boys and girls alike, the popular kids and the misfits. Knowing the power that came with praying the Scriptures, she prayed for Joshua according to 1 Thessalonians 5:15, that he would never "pay back wrong for wrong, but always try to be kind to everyone."

A few weeks later, Joshua came home from school with a story that, to Marlae, was an obvious answer to that specific prayer. He told how, earlier that day, a group of seventh graders had spent their break time playing in a field behind the school. The grass was fairly long in some places, and evidently there was a long stick or a stump poking out of the ground. All of a sudden, Joshua heard a sharp cry. Looking around, he saw the heaviest girl in his class sitting on the ground, holding her leg. She had hurt herself on the stick, and even from a distance he could tell that the wound was serious—blood covered the girl's hands and ran down to her shoe.

For a moment, nobody moved. Joshua hardly knew the girl, and as he looked at his friends, he could tell that they were as uncomfortable as he was. But he knew that he couldn't just stand there.

"Are you OK?" he asked, hurrying over to where the girl sat.

"No," she whimpered. "I can't walk."

"Well, we need to get you to the nurse's office," Joshua said. "Do you think you can climb onto my back?"

Wiping her tears on her sleeve, the girl nodded her head. She hoisted herself onto Joshua's back. He staggered for an instant and then regained his footing. Walking past his friends, he carried the girl into the school.

"Joshua," Marlae said, when her son finished the tale, "I am so proud of you. You did the right thing."

"Thanks, Mom," Joshua said a little sheepishly. "Do you think you can get the bloodstains out of these jeans? They're my favorite pair."

Marlae found herself smiling as she turned her attention back to her groceries. She pictured her son as a lanky thirteen-year-old, struggling under the weight of a classmate—and a *girl*, to boot! God certainly had a good sense of humor—and a beautiful way of answering a mother's prayers!

Poised for Prayer

I love Marlae's story because it shows how our hopes and desires for our kids' lives often remain unchanged, even as they grow up and mature. Marlae prayed that her son would be kind when he was just thirteen, and then—even as Joshua evidenced kindness and compassion in answer to those prayers—she continued to lay that request before God's throne. I wouldn't be surprised to see Marlae praying that very same prayer when Joshua is twenty-five or thirty, asking God to equip her son with a tenderness toward his wife or a genuine concern for his coworkers or his children. As praying parents, we can delight in asking God to keep the floodgates of blessing wide open throughout our children's lives!

I also love Marlae's story because it illustrates an important principle about faith. Very often, it is easier to ask God for something when we have already seen him move in answer to our prayers than when we are "flying blind"—living and praying by *faith* and not, as 2 Corinthians 5:7 puts it, by *sight*. When God shows up—as he did in answer to Marlae's prayer when Joshua was thirteen years old—it emboldens us to meet future prayer challenges with confidence and faith. We believe God because we have seen what he can do.

But what about those times when we don't have a "prayer precedent"? What if we haven't seen God work in answer to our prayers—or what if he allows something to happen that is definitely *not* the answer we were expecting or wanting? Where, then, do we place our faith?

The one place where we can put our trust—the one place where we can know that our faith will never be shaken—is in the character of God. Not in *what* he has done but in *who* he is. The Bible shows us a God who is good. It testifies to a God who is powerful. A God who is trustworthy, dependable, and unchanging. A God who loves us more than life itself—because he *is* love itself.

Prayer Principle

Faith enables us to pray with confidence—even when we cannot see God working—because our prayers are based not on what God has done but on who he is.

In Exodus 3:13, right after the Lord shows up in the burning bush, Moses asks God to tell him his name. I love how God identifies himself. He says, "I am who I am." And then, using capital letters, he repeats himself, saying, "This is what you are to say to the Israelites: 'I AM has sent me to you.'"

If you are looking for a place to put your faith today — whether you are praying through a relatively "low drama" season of your teen's life or a full-fledged crisis — put it in the God of Exodus 3:14, the One who is known as "I AM." Put it in the God of Psalm 145:13, the One who is "faithful to all his promises and loving toward all he has made." Put it in the God of Lamentations 3:22, the One whose mercy and compassion never fails. Put it in the God of Philippians 1:6, the One who promises that he will be faithful to bring to completion the good work he has begun in us — and in our teens.

Put your faith in the God who is.

Prayers You Can Use

Heavenly Father,

Thank you for the compassion that you have shown to us. I pray that _____ would follow your example, being compassionate and gracious, slow to anger, and abounding in love.   PSALM 103:8

Cause _____ to love even his enemies, doing good to them without expecting to get anything back. Let him obey your command to be merciful, just as you, Lord, are merciful.   LUKE 6:35 – 36

Comfort _____ in all her troubles, so that she may be ready and willing to comfort others in their time of need.

2 CORINTHIANS 1:4

Let _____ open his arms to the poor and extend his hands to the needy, honoring you by his kindness.

PROVERBS 31:20; 14:31

As _____ gets dressed each day, please clothe her with compassion, kindness, humility, gentleness, and patience.

COLOSSIANS 3:12

Let _____ be kind and compassionate to others, forgiving them, just as in Christ God forgave him. EPHESIANS 4:32

Fill _____ with your Holy Spirit, that her life might be marked by kindness, goodness, and joy. GALATIANS 5:22

Strengthen _____ so that he will not become weary in doing good. Let him recognize opportunities to show kindness and compassion, doing good to all people—especially to those who belong to the family of believers.

GALATIANS 6:9–10

As _____ grows in her relationship with you, give her an undivided heart and a new spirit. Take away any hard and stony attitudes and replace them with a heart of flesh, that she may be tender toward you, Lord, and toward others.

EZEKIEL 11:19

May _____ live in harmony with his siblings, his friends, and his teammates. Let him be sympathetic, compassionate, and humble. I PETER 3:8

Anoint _____ , just as you anointed Jesus, so that she will go around doing good and bringing your help and healing touch to others. ACTS 10:38

Let _____ show mercy and compassion to others, especially to orphans, foreigners, poor people, and others in great need. ZECHARIAH 7:9–10

CHAPTER 6

Praying about
Your Teen's Attire

Your beauty should not come from outward adornment,
such as ... the wearing of gold jewelry and fine clothes.
Instead, it should be that of your inner self, the unfading beauty
of a gentle and quiet spirit, which is of great worth in God's sight.

1 PETER 3:3–4

Three teenage girls live in our house. They share the same gene pool, but when it comes to getting dressed in the morning, you would think that they came from different planets.

One daughter chooses classic, somewhat unremarkable, clothing—solid color tops paired with solid color skirts or slacks. Her low-risk fashion strategy means that she is almost never late to breakfast, and—unlike her three siblings—she has never been cited for a dress code violation at school.

Another daughter likes to accessorize her outfits, and she sets it all out before she goes to bed each night—complete with shoes, belts, necklaces, and hair ribbons, all arranged in the way that they will look once they are actually on her body. Walking into her darkened room, I have been startled by her artistry more than once. If you didn't know better, you would swear she had a corpse on the floor.

The third daughter—and I am purposely not telling you who's who—gets dressed each day as though she has been given two minutes to evacuate. The clothing flies everywhere, and she must try on five or six different outfits before breakfast—and another two or three after that. Looking at the carnage of her closet, I am often tempted to call in a FEMA crew.

I marvel at my kids, but if I am to be honest, I have to admit that I, too, often struggle with the "what to wear" question. And this isn't just a girl thing: apparently, even the disciples spent some time wondering about their clothing. I love the fact that Jesus deemed their concerns important enough to address—and even more than that, I love the wisdom of his straightforward advice:

> "Don't worry about everyday life—whether you have enough food to eat or clothes to wear. For life consists of far more than food and clothing....
>
> Look at the lilies and how they grow. They don't work or make their clothing, yet Solomon in all his glory was not dressed as beautifully as they are. And if God cares so wonderfully for flowers that are here today and gone tomorrow, won't he more surely care for you?"
>
> LUKE 12:22–23, 27–28 NLT

Wouldn't it be great if we could get our teens—and for that matter, ourselves—to take the Lord's words to heart? Imagine knowing that the prom or a party was coming up, and being able to trust God to provide the perfect dress. That's exactly what happened to a mom named Laurie, shortly after her family moved from the Seattle area to a new home in Iowa ...

Laurie heard the front door open. Closing the document on her computer, she turned to see her fifteen-year-old daughter, Aimee, put her book bag on the kitchen table. From the way her teen was standing, Laurie could tell that something was wrong. She knew that, as a new student, Aimee was still looking for ways to forge relationships with the other kids, and she hoped that nothing had happened to make Aimee feel left out.

"How was school today?" she prompted.

"Fine. But you know the dinner that the church is hosting on Saturday night?"

"Mm-hmm."

"All the girls are getting together at Stacy's house to get dressed beforehand. They invited me to come over and get ready with them."

Right away, Laurie understood Aimee's concern. The dinner was to be a formal affair, and Aimee—having never been to a formal anything—had nothing to wear. Not wanting to spend a lot of money on a dress that would probably be worn only once, Laurie had emailed several friends to see whether they had something that her daughter might be able to borrow. So far, though, she had come up empty. And, with the dinner just three days away, she knew that they were running out of time.

Even if someone did have a dress to lend, the odds were slim that it would fit Aimee's figure in an attractive way. Laurie was no prude, but she didn't want her daughter going to a church-sponsored event in one of the scanty dresses that seemed to be so popular with the teenage crowd. Not only that, but Aimee's coloring—green eyes, auburn hair, and porcelain skin—left her with a limited palette when it came to the colors that she found herself eager to wear.

For a teen, Aimee was remarkably mature in her outlook. Never once had she complained about not having a formal dress, and she had even gone so far as to count her blessings, knowing full well that there were people in the world who had little or no clothing of any kind. But Laurie's heart ached for her daughter. She knew that, like most girls, Aimee didn't always feel good about her appearance, and Laurie yearned to give her what she called a "beauty boost."

"Aimee," she said, "I know that God cares about even the little stuff like formal dresses. Let's ask him to send us a dress."

"Mom, the dinner is on Saturday!"

"I know that. But let's ask him anyway."

Later that night, Laurie shared her concern with the Lord. "Father God," she prayed, "I realize that this formal dinner is not a monumental thing. But if Aimee is going to go, she needs a dress. Would you please send her one? I know it would encourage her faith, and if she could get together beforehand with the other girls, it would really help her adjust to our new home and feel like she has some good friends. You are so creative, God—I know that you can help us."

The next morning, Laurie awoke to a blanket of white. Another Iowa snowstorm had turned their neighborhood into a winter wonderland and, Laurie realized, left them stranded. Laurie fixed a pot of coffee and called the city, asking them to send a snowplow as soon as they could.

Holding her steaming mug, Laurie looked out the window. Suddenly, she noticed an unfamiliar car parked on the street. She realized that it would be directly in the path of the snow-plow. Laurie had no idea whose car it was, but, donning her heaviest coat and a pair of sturdy boots, she aimed to find out.

After knocking on several doors, Laurie found the car's owner. It belonged to the friend of a teen named Chantel, whose mother, Weiss, invited Laurie to come inside and out of the cold. Laurie told Weiss that she, too, had a teenage daughter.

"She has this big dinner tomorrow night," Laurie said. "It's at our church—but so far, Aimee has nothing to wear."

"What's the attire?" Weiss asked.

"It's supposed to be formal. Aimee has never been to anything that fancy before."

"Come upstairs," Weiss said. "I have something to show you."

Laurie followed her neighbor up the stairs and into a bed-room. Weiss opened the closet. There, a single dress hung.

"That's Aimee's favorite color!" Laurie gasped. "It's gorgeous!"

The dress was a pale, shimmery, sage green—just like Ai-mee's eyes. It hung almost all the way to the floor, and even on its hanger, Laurie could tell that the drape of the fabric was beautiful.

"Look," Weiss said, "the price tags are still attached. I bought this for Chantel, but she's never worn it. The color is just not right for her. Do you think Aimee would like it?"

Laurie knew that Aimee would love the dress, but she wondered how much it had cost. When she saw the tags, though, her heart skipped a beat. Not only was the dress Aimee's exact size, but it was remarkably affordable.

"I bought it on sale a few months ago," Weiss explained. "You are welcome to it if you want it."

Carrying the dress back through the snow, Laurie wanted to laugh out loud. Long before they had ever moved to Iowa, God had known that this Saturday night would be special for Aimee. And when Aimee slipped the dress over her head, standing back to look at her reflection in the mirror, there could be no doubt: The dress was never meant to be worn by Chantel; it was intended for Aimee, the new girl in town, the one who needed to know that God loved her and thought she was beautiful.

Prayer Principle

God loves your teen, and he cares about
even the smallest details in her life.

Poised for Prayer

I love knowing that God cares about something as seemingly inconsequential as clothing. And the Bible is full of fashion commentary. Consider the runway models described in Isaiah 3. The women of Zion, this chapter says, had bangles and headbands and necklaces. They wore earrings and bracelets and veils. They adorned themselves with ankle chains, sashes, and charms, and they put rings on their fingers and through their noses. They carried perfume bottles and purses and mirrors. They wore linen garments, tiaras, and shawls. And over it all, they put on fine robes, capes, and cloaks.[1]

And I thought *we* were short on closet space!

The ladies of Zion may have looked fantastic, but God saw beyond the bangles. He says they were "haughty, walking along with outstretched necks, flirting with their eyes, tripping along with mincing steps, with ornaments jingling on their ankles." God saw their proud, rebellious hearts — and in response, he vowed to put sores on their heads and make them go bald.[2] Now there's a story angle that I bet the editors of *Vogue* haven't considered!

Throughout the pages of Scripture, clothing is often linked with character. It's no secret that the way we dress sends a message about who we are and what we value. I'm not sure how much the apostle Paul knew about fashion, but he certainly offered plenty of dress code pointers for those who profess to follow Christ. Here are some examples:

- "Clothe yourselves with the Lord Jesus Christ," Paul writes in Romans 13:14, "and do not think about how to gratify the desires of the sinful nature." *Translation: If your aim is to please God, dress like you mean it.*
- "Don't copy the behavior and customs of this world," he writes in Romans 12:2 (NLT). *Translation: Just because the kids in your school dress like hoochy mamas doesn't mean that you should.*
- Or how about this one from Paul's letter to Timothy: "I also want women to dress modestly, with decency and propriety, not with braided hair or gold or pearls or

---

1. Isaiah 3:18 – 23.   2. Isaiah 3:16 – 17.

expensive clothes, but with good deeds, appropriate for women who profess to worship God."[1] *Translation: Your attention should be devoted to godly deeds, not to the way you look.*

In her book *Your Girl: Raising a Godly Daughter in an Ungodly World*, author Vicky Courtney notes that when Paul wrote about fashion in his letter to Timothy, he was not just cautioning against immodesty but against anything that "would serve to distract from God during a worship service."[2] Reading these words, I couldn't help but recall the Communion service we attended where a woman walked up to the altar with a purse slung over her shoulder that looked just like the *Titanic*. It had all of the smokestacks and everything. My daughters and I were trying (although not very hard, I guess) to focus on the Lord, but as soon as we saw that handbag, we were doomed. I'm not saying that it was wrong for the woman to carry such an intriguing purse; I share this story merely to show how easily we can be distracted by fashion.

And, truth be told, eye-popping purses are nothing when it comes to the wide range of wardrobe malfunctions that can lure our eyeballs today. For instance, underwear is no longer *under* anything. Bra straps, thong straps, you name it — garments we once tried to hide are now *designed* to be seen. And it's not just a girl thing. A group of middle school boys recently told me that showing their boxer shorts was part of their "identity," with plaid versus plain sending an integral message about who they are. I wish I could say that kids from Christian families

---

1. 1 Timothy 2:9.   2. Vicky Courtney, *Your Girl: Raising a Godly Daughter in an Ungodly World* (Nashville: Broadman & Holman, 2004), 105.

dressed with more decorum than their secular counterparts, but I've worked with church youth groups and teen ministries for the past five years, and I can tell you that "our" kids don't look a whole lot different that "theirs." As parents, what are we thinking?

We aren't, I'm afraid. We have—knowingly or not—bought into a culture that uses clothing to say, "Look at me!" We allow our kids to dress in ways that please their peers—rarely stopping to think about whether or not their attire will please God. We tell ourselves that it's OK, that it's no big deal, that it's just how "everyone" dresses these days. Without even realizing it, we are following in the footsteps of the women of Zion.

But it doesn't have to be that way. Let's pray that God would open our eyes—and our kids' eyes—so that we can see the clothing of our culture the way that he sees it. Because parents and teens often have very different perspectives on style, let's also ask for divine discernment so that we can spot the difference between clothing that is merely *ugly* (and not worth arguing over) and that which is *immodest*. Most of all, let's ask the Lord to change our hearts so that, instead of dressing to fit in with the world or draw attention to *ourselves*, we will clothe ourselves with Christ, letting all that we say and do and wear shine the spotlight on *him*.

Clothing is a big deal to teens, and when we take the time to pray about what they wear—whether they simply need a dress for a dance or a full-scale attitude adjustment in the "Look at me!" department—we invite God to demonstrate his power and his provision in their lives. After all, if God cares enough to outfit the lilies, we can be sure that he cares about our kids.

Prayers You Can Use

Heavenly Father,

Clothe _____ with the Lord Jesus Christ. Let him be decent and true in all that he does, so that he will not spend time thinking about ways to gratify the desires of his sinful nature.   ROMANS 13:14

Clothe _____ with strength and dignity. Help her remember that charm is deceptive, and beauty is fleeting, but a woman who fears the Lord is to be praised.

PROVERBS 31:25, 30

Cause _____ to be dressed ready for service and to be well prepared and always watching for your Son's return.

LUKE 12:35

Let _____ be clothed with Christ, that the Spirit of God might come upon him even as you came on Gideon, wrapping yourself around him like a garment so that he was able to lead others in wisdom and righteousness.

GALATIANS 3:27; JUDGES 6:34

Teach _____ how to dress modestly. Let her be eager to wear decent and appropriate clothing so that she will not draw attention to herself or cause others to stumble into sin as they look at her.   1 TIMOTHY 2:9; 1 CORINTHIANS 10:32

Whether or not _____ has plenty of clothing, let him be content in every situation.   PHILIPPIANS 4:12

Let _____'s attractiveness come from her good deeds rather than from any jewelry or expensive clothing that she wears.   1 TIMOTHY 2:9–10

Clothe _____ with joy, and let his heart sing to you.   PSALM 30:11–12

Don't let _____ be like a haughty woman of Zion, walking around with an outstretched neck and flirtatious eyes. Instead, cause her to clothe herself with humility, knowing that you oppose the proud but give grace to the humble.   ISAIAH 3:16; 1 PETER 5:5

Whether _____ needs sports equipment, school clothing, new shoes, or even a tuxedo, help him to rely on you, knowing that you are the God who promises to meet all of his needs according to your glorious riches in Christ Jesus.   PHILIPPIANS 4:19

Help _____ not to worry about or focus on what she wears. Point her eyes toward the beauty of your creation, and remind her that if you know how to clothe even the grass of the field, you can certainly provide beautiful clothing for her.   MATTHEW 6:28–30

Please crown _____ with your beauty, covering him with the oil of gladness instead of mourning and a garment of praise instead of a spirit of despair.   ISAIAH 61:3

You, Lord, are enthralled by _____'s beauty. Let her honor you by what she wears and by all that she says and does.   PSALM 45:11

As _____ leaves our house each day, clothe him with the sturdy belt of truth and the body armor of your righteousness. Let him wear shoes that are ready to preach the Good News of peace. Give him the shield of faith to stop Satan's fiery arrows, and adorn his head with the helmet of salvation. Let him carry and use the sword of the Spirit, which is your word.   EPHESIANS 6:14–17

PART 2

PRAYING
for Your TEEN'S
RELATIONSHIPS

CHAPTER 7

Praying for Your Teen's Relationship with You

Children, obey your parents in everything,
for this pleases the Lord. Fathers, do not embitter your children,
or they will become discouraged.
COLOSSIANS 3:20–21

In the 2003 movie *Cheaper by the Dozen*, there's a scene in which actor Steve Martin (playing the dad) confronts his son "Charlie" about a missed curfew, his girlfriend, and his plans for college — none of which Charlie seems all that eager to discuss. In the end, Martin asks Charlie if there is anything else he would like to talk about.

"Have I mentioned that I don't like you very much?" Charlie says.

"You mentioned that," Martin acknowledges.

"Then I'm good," Charlie says, with a smile on his face.

I love this scene because, while it's clear that father and son love each other, it's equally obvious that they are not on the same wavelength. You don't need to be a family psychologist to know that parents and teens often see things very differently — and even in families where folks truly love each other, there will be times when you might not *like* each other all that much.

We live in a culture that tends to eye the parent-teen relationship with a mixture of fear and uncertainty. When conflict happens—as it inevitably does—we often point at our teens, fingering them as the source of the problem. After all, they are the ones with the raging hormones and all the attitudes, right?

Right—and wrong. Teens have attitudes—nobody says that they don't—but so do we. And before we go saddling our kids with blame, we need to turn the mirror on ourselves. In his book *Age of Opportunity*, Paul David Tripp says that the teen years are often hard for parents because "they expose the wrong thoughts and desires of our *own* hearts"—things like self-righteousness, impatience, and a desire for our kids to succeed so that *we* will look good.[1]

Ouch. No wonder our daughter Hillary says she wants to write *Praying the Scriptures for Your Parents*.

I'm sure that the experts could come up with all sorts of contributing factors for the tension that often colors the parent-teen relationship, but as I've conducted my own informal research—which basically consists of talking to other moms—an issue that seems to crop up again and again is the parent's need for control. I know that our teens have their own hearts to tame, but as I look at what we parents can do to improve the climate in our homes, being willing to "let go and let God" is certainly part of the package. Every other chapter in this book centers on our teens and the issues they face; I want to take a few pages now to turn the spotlight on us.

Leslie is a mother I know only through email. Like me, she has three girls and one boy. Like me, too, she finds herself having to make what can feel like a million little decisions every

---

1. Paul David Tripp, *Age of Opportunity* (Phillipsburg, N.J.: P & R, 2001), 17–18.

day: Can I go to the concert? Can I sleep at John's house? Can I borrow the car? Can I go to Sally's party? Can I ...?

*Un*like me, though, Leslie has learned to trust God to help her know when to hold her ground and when to let go. And in a world filled with tug-of-war issues, letting God call the shots can make all the difference ...

"That's not fair!" Sara Kay cried, a look of anguish crossing her pretty face. "It's my senior prom!"

"I realize that, honey," Leslie answered calmly. "But it is also your sister's college graduation. You went to the prom last year. This year, we are going—as a family—to be with Rebecca. Case closed."

Sara Kay stomped off, and Leslie thought she'd heard the end of it. Two weeks later, though, Sara Kay skipped into the kitchen. "Riley asked me to go to prom with him!" she exclaimed.

"What did you tell him?" Leslie queried.

"I said yes, of course!"

"Sara Kay," Leslie said reprovingly, "You know how much we all like Riley. But you can't go with him. In case you've forgotten, we're all going to be up at Rebecca's graduation."

"But, Mom," Sara Kay protested, "I talked to Rebecca and she said she doesn't mind if I go to prom."

"That's what she says now. But down the road, she might feel differently. Prom happens every year, and you've gone before. Rebecca will only graduate from college once."

"But the dance is on Saturday night. I could fly up on Sunday morning and be with the family for Rebecca's ceremony. Pleeeeease, Mom!"

"Listen, Sara Kay. As far as I'm concerned, this subject is not open for discussion. You can talk to God about it if you want, but I am not changing my mind unless he intervenes. Now go tell Riley that you can't go with him so that he'll have time to ask someone else."

Sara Kay did talk to Riley—and to God. Meanwhile, Leslie found herself wondering if she had made the right decision. She had nothing against the prom, and Riley was a family friend who would certainly be a safe and courteous date—but didn't her daughter realize that a college graduation was more important than a dance? Her husband seemed open to the idea of letting Sara Kay go to the prom; was she making a mistake by insisting that the family stay together for the entire graduation weekend? "God," she prayed silently, "let me be open to whatever you want for Sara Kay."

The next few days were a whirlwind of change and activity. A neighbor—who had been wanting to attend the graduation anyway—offered to travel with Sara Kay, and they managed to find a cheap flight that would get them to the school in time for the ceremony. Another neighbor said that Sara Kay could spend the night with her after the dance. For her part, Sara Kay agreed to skip the after-prom parties and promised to be home by midnight. Leslie felt the reins of control slipping out of her fingertips, but—somewhat to her surprise—it didn't matter. She realized that God had changed her heart.

And when her cell phone rang late on prom night, it all made sense. "Mom," Sara Kay said, her voice breathless with excitement, "Guess what?"

"What?"

"I was chosen as prom queen! And Riley was the king!"

Leslie thought she might drop the phone. Making her daughter miss the prom would have been one thing; making her miss being the queen—a once-in-a-lifetime event—would have been something else entirely. And God had known all along what would happen!

"God taught me a wonderful family lesson," Leslie told me later. "By trusting him and being open to his intervention, we avoided the guilt and resentment that could have cropped up had I insisted that we do things the way that made sense to me. I learned that if we seek the Lord in our family decisions, letting him reign instead of always trying to be in control all by ourselves, he will keep us from making really big mistakes."

Poised for Prayer

As a mom who does not like to give up control, I love the lessons in Leslie's story. I love that she asked the Lord to soften her heart—something she could not do on her own. I love that she taught her daughter to bring her concerns to God—thereby nourishing a prayer relationship that Sara Kay can rely on throughout her life. And I love what she said about being open to God's intervention, even when it didn't make sense to her. As God reminds us in Isaiah 55:8, his thoughts are not our thoughts, and his ways are not our ways. They are—as the NLT puts it—"completely different" and "far beyond anything [we] could imagine."

Happily for us, God took the time to make many of his thoughts clear to us through the pages of Scripture. There may not be a formula for creating the perfect parent-teen relationship, but the verses at the beginning of this chapter—Colossians 3:20–21—is a pretty good place to start. The first part—where God tells children to obey their parents—is one of those commands that gets repeated over and over again in the Bible. God introduces the concept of filial honor in the fifth commandment—"honor your father and your mother"—and then he repeats the charge in Leviticus, Deuteronomy, Proverbs, Matthew, Mark, Colossians, and Ephesians.[1] Not only does God take the honoring thing pretty seriously, but he adds that when children honor and obey their parents, they will reap a "long life, full of blessing."[2]

When we pray that our teens will honor us, we are not being selfish or controlling. Rather, we are opening the door to a lifetime of God's best!

(If your kids aren't the type to be motivated by promises like a life full of blessing, you can always try the opposite approach. Point them toward helpful verses like Proverbs 30:17: "The eye that mocks a father, that scorns obedience to a mother, will be pecked out by the ravens of the valley, will be eaten by the vultures." Talk about your inspirational passages!)

Prayer Principle

When we pray that our teens
will honor and obey us,
we are opening the door to a lifetime
of God's blessing.

---

1. Exodus 20:12; Leviticus 19:3; Deuteronomy 5:16; 27:16; Proverbs 1:8; 23:22; Matthew 15:4; Mark 7:10; Colossians 3:20–21; Ephesians 6:2–3.
2. See Exodus 20:12; Ephesians 6:3 NLT.

As we pray for our teens to honor us, let's not forget the second part of the Colossian charge: "Fathers [and mothers], do not embitter your children, or they will become discouraged." God wants us to teach and correct and raise our teens with a spirit of love, taking care not to aggravate or provoke them, lest they decide to quit trying.

A tall order? You bet. But as we seek God's wisdom for the daily decisions of our lives, parenting in the way that he directs and being willing to extend grace to our kids in the same measure that God gives it to us, he will make a way. He is the God of Malachi 4:6, the only One who can turn the hearts of parents to their children, and the hearts of children to their parents.

Turn our hearts, O Lord.

Prayers You Can Use

Heavenly Father,

As a parent, help me to preach your word, and to be prepared in season and out of season. Show me how to correct, rebuke, and encourage my teen—with great patience and careful instruction.   2 Timothy 4:2

Teach me how to set a godly example for _____, and equip him to be like King Solomon, who as a young man walked before you in integrity of heart and uprightness, even as his father David did.   1 Kings 9:4

As _____ and I talk with each other, let no unwholesome talk come out of our mouths, but only what is helpful for building each other up according to our needs, that our words would benefit each other and strengthen our relationship.

Ephesians 4:29

Cause _____ to obey me, Lord, for this is right. Let him grab hold of the promise that comes with this commandment, that it may go well with him and that he may enjoy long life on this earth.   Ephesians 6:1–3

I pray that _____ would always listen to her father and not forsake her mother's teaching, so that these things will be a beautiful garland to grace her head.   Proverbs 1:8–9

Help me to train _____ in the way he should go, counting on your promise that when he is old he will not turn from it.   PROVERBS 22:6

Cause _____ to obey all your commands — including the one about honoring her parents — so that your joy will be in her and her joy will be complete. Let us love each other in the same self-sacrificing way you have loved us, dear Jesus.   JOHN 15:10–12

As I raise _____, please be my shepherd and lead me, Lord. Gather me in your arms and carry me close to your heart, giving me grace and wisdom as you gently lead "those that have young."   ISAIAH 40:11

Make _____ like John the Baptist, a son who brought joy and delight to his parents. Let him bring others back to you, Lord, turning the hearts of fathers to their children and the disobedient to the wisdom of the righteous.   LUKE 1:14–17

Let _____ be wise and keep her heart on the right path. Cause her to listen to her father, who gave her life. Please don't let _____ despise me when I am old (and not so old!).   PROVERBS 23:19, 22

Turn my heart toward _____, and turn his heart toward me.   MALACHI 4:6

CHAPTER 8

Praying for Good Friends

Two people are better off than one,
for they can help each other succeed.
If one person falls,
the other can reach out and help ...
A person standing alone
can be attacked and defeated,
but two can stand back-to-back and conquer.
ECCLESIASTES 4:9 – 10, 12 NLT

When Robbie was about six or seven years old, I tiptoed into his room late one night to give him a kiss. I was surprised — and concerned — to find him awake. He was sobbing silently, the tears streaming down his sweet little cheeks.

"What is it?" I asked, feeling to see whether he had a fever. "What's the matter?"

"It's just so sad to think about you having to eat lunch all alone every day at school," he said. "I feel so sorry for you."

I couldn't believe it. Some time earlier — I couldn't even remember when — I had told my kids about my experience in middle school. To say that I was not one of the popular kids would be putting it gently; truth be told, my only real friend had moved away the summer before, and I spent almost all of my eighth grade year scanning the hallways for someone—anyone—who would meet my eyes and return my hopeful greeting. I didn't get many takers, and more often than not, I worked my way through the lunch line and tried to find a spot to sit down where I wouldn't be in anyone's way. There were plenty of days when I ate my lunch alone.

I'm not sure if there's any connection, but I also carried a big brown leather purse engraved with the words "Jesus is Lord." All of the cool girls had brown leather purses, and I had begged my parents to get me one, too. How was I supposed to know that they got a discount at the Christian bookstore? The other girls' purses were small and delicate—but then they could afford to be, since theirs didn't bear any messages or engravings, other than a few dainty flowers.

Another unique feature of my bag was that it came with an imposing padlock—apparently, I suppose, to discourage those who didn't fully believe that Jesus is Lord from stealing my stuff. Looking back, I can't believe I carried that purse to school every day, but I did. Somewhere along the line, I had memorized the verse where Jesus says, "If anyone is ashamed of me . . . , the Son of Man will be ashamed of him when he comes in his Father's glory with the holy angels,"[1] and I guess I wasn't taking any chances.

I may not have had many friends at school—and certainly none who would have joined me in professing Christ's lordship—but during the summer months, everything changed. Each year, we attended a Christian family camp, where I hung out with an eclectic group of teens from several states. They

---

1. Mark 8:38.

all loved the Lord, and the weeks we spent at the camp, along with the weekends during the school year when we visited each other by hopping on trains and buses, were the absolute highlight of my middle school years. In an era before things like cell phones and instant messaging, my camp friends and I stayed in touch by—and my kids think I'm making this up—writing letters to each other pretty much every single day.[1]

I suppose that my life would have gone on like that forever—waiting like a rabid dog for the mail carrier to appear—except that my parents started praying. They asked God to send me a Christian friend and fervently hoped that a Bible-believing family might move to town. But God had better plans. Unbeknownst to my folks, on the very day they started praying, one of the local churches began planning an evangelistic event that wound up transforming our community—teens included. Suddenly, there were a whole slew of kids who wanted to get to know Jesus and who—miracle of miracles—wanted to eat lunch with *me*. It was like some made-for-TV Disney movie, only better!

My friend Isabelle would appreciate this story. Like my folks, she desperately wanted the Lord to bring a godly friend into her teen's life ...

"Why don't you invite some kids over tonight?" Isabelle offered, as her sixteen-year-old son Brian helped her unload the groceries from her car. "I bought a bunch of soft drinks, and we could order a pizza."

---

1. My parents didn't know it, but family experts—ranging from Dr. James Dobson to the mother of five who sits a few rows behind me at church—say that sending a teen to a Christian camp is one of the best financial investments that a parent can make in a child. The appendix in the back of this book contains a listing of several Christ-centered camps that are specially designed for teens.

"Aw, Mom, nobody wants to do that."

"What do you mean? Why *wouldn't* they want to come over?"

"Nobody wants to be where they know that the parents are watching," Brian replied. "Plus, all the kids know that you and Dad don't allow any drinking. Thanks anyway, but I'll pass on the party."

Isabelle sighed, hating the fact that her kids were growing up in a culture where such things as drinking and sex were considered a normal part of adolescent life. She and her husband, Craig, had been very clear about their expectations for Brian's conduct—and for the most part, he had lived up to them. Now that Brian was preparing to enter his junior year in high school, however, the temptations seemed greater than ever. In addition to alcohol and girlfriends, Isabelle found herself concerned about even simple things such as unkind words and inappropriate music and movies. "Whatever Brian does," she often prayed, using the words of Colossians 3:23, "let him work at it with all his heart, as working for you, Lord, and not to please people."

Being a people-pleaser, Isabelle knew, was yet another temptation for her son. Like most teens, he valued the friendship and opinions of his peers, and on more than one occasion, Isabelle found herself having to—as she puts it—"put myself in the way" to prevent Brian from making too many mistakes. Sometimes the boundaries Isabelle set meant that Brian was left out of parties and other social events—and during those times, she knew that her son felt the loneliness keenly. She prayed that God would send just one friend into his life—just one!—who would share his faith and help hold him accountable in terms of doing things that would please the Lord. So far, though, Isabelle didn't see anyone on the horizon who fit that description.

Instead, her radar screen was filled with kids like Jarred, a fellow who had put himself on the "one to watch" list when the boys were relatively young. Jarred's older brothers had exposed him to movies, computer games, and Internet sites that Isabelle did not approve of, and when he began to share his discoveries with Brian, she drew the line. "Jarred can come to our house anytime you like," she said to Brian, "but you are no longer allowed to go over there."

As the boys grew, Jarred began experimenting with sex, drinking, and drugs. By the time they hit high school, he had earned a fairly tarnished reputation among the school's faculty and on the parental grapevine. Even Jarred's standing among his peers — kids who had once looked to him as a leader — had begun to fade. Brian understood why his mom had wanted him to put some distance between himself and Jarred, so it didn't make much sense when he saw her hugging him after a football game.

"Do you *like* Jarred?" Brian asked later that night.

"Of course!" Isabelle responded. "You guys have been friends since you were little kids, you've played sports together forever, and now you're on the same football team! How could I *not* like Jarred?"

"But, Mom," Brian persisted, "I don't get it. Sometimes you seem so judgmental — like when you won't let me spend the night at Jarred's house — and sometimes you seem so cool."

"Brian," Isabelle said slowly, "this may be hard to understand, but when your friends look at me, I want them to see

Jesus and his love, not just some judgmental, overprotective parent. I know that Jarred has made some pretty big mistakes — and that's why I don't let you do everything that he and some of the other kids do — but the bottom line is that I want to love your friends and encourage them, and I'm asking God to help me do that."

Loving and encouraging Brian's friends was the right thing to do — Isabelle had no doubt about that. The thing she sometimes questioned, though, was whether it was wise for her to prevent Brian from doing the things that he wanted to do. After all, he would be in college in two years. If she kept putting herself in the way of potentially bad friendships and decisions, would he be prepared for the choices he would have to make when he was on his own? She needed God's wisdom to know when to hold her son back and when to let him go.

Isabelle knew that the year ahead would be a critical one. Brian would be stepping onto the football field as the team's starting quarterback — a position that afforded him an unprecedented opportunity for influence. Kids who once looked to Jarred to call the shots were starting to look to Brian for leadership. It was a subtle shift, but one that did not go unnoticed in Isabelle's eyes. Time — and God — certainly had a way of turning things around.

When one of the football coaches approached Brian about starting a Fellowship of Christian Athletes group for his teammates, Isabelle sensed that God was doing something that went beyond her expectations.[1] She had prayed that God would send a Christian friend to help him stand strong; now it looked

---

1. For more information on the Fellowship of Christian Athletes, please visit the website at www.fca.org.

as though God could be planning to use Brian as one who would encourage other kids. Eager to align her prayers with God's purposes, Isabelle broadened the scope of her request. "Let Brian live wisely among those who are not Christians," she prayed, using the words of Colossians 4:5, "and help him to make the most of every opportunity."

Like most of the stories in this book, Brian's is still being written. Isabelle has clearly seen God's hand at work—both in protecting her son from negative influences and in elevating him to a position of leadership among his peers—and she is grateful. She still wants godly friends to surround her son—what praying parent wouldn't?—but she is willing to let God work things out according to his plan.

Poised for Prayer

I would love to introduce Isabelle to my friend Cindy. Cindy says that she prayed that her teens would be surrounded by "people of good influence"—until she looked around and realized that the pickings were rather slim on that front. Not one to get easily discouraged, she adjusted her prayer tactic slightly, asking instead that her kids would *be* people of good influence.

Cindy's daughter got married not long ago. We went to the wedding, and I wish I could put her picture here on this page. Words could not possibly describe the joy, the life, the *vibrancy*, that this young woman radiated—and not just the bride but the whole pack of bridesmaids and groomsmen and the entourage of friends who crowded onto the dance floor. "Slim pickings" had turned into a bountiful harvest—almost every one of these young people had professed faith in Christ, and it showed! God had answered Cindy's prayers with an abundance that exceeded her wildest dreams.

From the emails I received while working on this book, the "friends" issue is a huge prayer concern. Some of you are asking God to bring godly friends into your teen's life; others just want to see God get rid of some of the bad kids. Either way, Scripture is brimming with promises that will fill your heart with hope.

I remember going to God after one of our family's cross-country moves, at a time when it felt as though one of our girls had no one she could really count on for encouragement and support. "She just needs a friend!" I found myself crying out to the Lord.

I opened my Bible to John 15, and the words practically jumped off the page. "There is no greater love," verse 13 (NLT) read, "than to lay down one's life for one's friends. You are my friends—*and* she *is my friend*—if you do what I command. I no longer call you slaves.... Now you are my friends."

There it was. The Lord himself had promised to walk beside my daughter and to be her friend.

He does that for our kids. Teenage friends may come and go, but the Lord will never, ever, stop loving our teens—nor will he abandon them. Deuteronomy 31:6 puts it like this: "The LORD your God goes with you; he will never leave you nor forsake you."

Prayer Principle

Teenage friends may come and go, but the Lord will
never abandon your child.

As we pray for our teens, let's remind them of God's immeasurable love—and his absolute faithfulness—as often as we can. Let's also encourage them to look for ways to *give* love and acceptance to their peers—even though they might be more inclined to focus on *receiving* it. As Isabelle and Cindy did, let's ask God to help our kids reach out to others with love, standing strong in the face of peer pressure and temptation. It might look like slim pickings on your teen's social horizon right now, but don't despair. Instead, keep praying, remembering Paul's charge in Galatians 6:9: "Let us not become weary in doing good, for at the proper time we will reap a harvest if we do not give up."

Prayers You Can Use

Heavenly Father,

Surround _____ with good friends — those who will sharpen him as iron sharpens iron.   PROVERBS 27:17

Prompt _____ to pursue faith and love and peace, and let her enjoy the companionship of those who call on you out of a pure heart.   2 TIMOTHY 2:22

Don't allow _____ to follow the crowd in doing wrong.   EXODUS 23:2

You promise to extend your friendship to those who fear you. Be _____'s friend, and share the secrets of your covenant with him. Cause him to look to you whenever he needs help.   PSALM 25:14–15

Don't let _____ exclude her peers or participate in gossip, since a perverse person stirs up dissension, and a gossip separates close friends.   PROVERBS 16:28

Count _____ as one of your friends. Let him love others with the same self-sacrificing love you have shown to him, being willing to lay down all that he has for his friends. Confide in _____, and let him find his security in the fact that you have chosen him as a friend.

JOHN 15:12–15

Use _____ to spread the fragrance of the knowledge of you. Let her be the aroma of Christ and of life to those around her. 2 CORINTHIANS 2:15–16

Teach _____ how to show love even to his enemies and to pray for kids who may reject him or persecute him. Remind him that if he is kind only to his friends, then he is no different from anyone else. MATTHEW 5:44–47

Don't let _____ pay back evil for evil, but cause her to focus on forgiveness, which breaks down walls between friends and restores relationships. GENESIS 50:14–21

Let _____ walk in the light of your presence and enjoy fellowship with other teens who love you. 1 JOHN 1:7

When _____ wrestles with loneliness or rejection, remind him of your promise: Though the mountains be shaken and the hills be removed, your unfailing love for him will never be shaken, nor will you remove your covenant of peace from his life.   ISAIAH 54:10

When _____ feels like her friends have rejected or deserted her, remind her that you are a friend who sticks closer than anyone.   PROVERBS 18:24

Equip _____ to speak the truth to his friends in love, supporting them and building them up by all that he says and does.   EPHESIANS 4:15 – 16

Send _____ a friend who will be her partner in spreading the Good News about Jesus Christ. Let them pray for one another, giving joyful thanks to you for the gift of their friendship.   PHILIPPIANS 1:3 – 5

CHAPTER 9

Praying for
Involvement in Church

Let us not give up meeting together,
as some are in the habit of doing,
but let us encourage one another—
and all the more
as you see the Day approaching.

HEBREWS 10:25

For the past several years, I have led a weekly Bible study for middle school girls. Somewhere along the line, the youth leaders at our church wisely decided that the girls would enjoy having an older teen in the mix, so that it wasn't just them and an "old lady" getting together every week. They partnered me with a beautiful redhead named Cally, a high school junior who knew how to do pretty much everything—from making beaded bracelets out of lengths of twine to dishing out godly advice on boys, schoolwork, sports, and a host of other life-and-death teenage concerns.

Like the girls, I quickly fell in love with Cally, and when the time came for her to apply to college, I couldn't wait to see what God had planned. Her first choice was Princeton University. I figured that the school had about a jillion highly qualified applicants, but after reading one of the essays on Cally's application, I didn't see how *any* school could turn her down.

The essay centered around a boy whom Cally had met in Thailand, a young survivor of the tsunami that had claimed the lives of more than two hundred thousand people in December 2004. She'd been in the country with a handful of teens from our church—kids who had seen the devastation on the news and wanted to help the Thai people rebuild their lives. It was a daunting task, but for Cally, mission work was nothing new: in summers past, she had taught English in China and helped run a vacation Bible school in the Dominican Republic.

Princeton must have liked the looks of Cally as much as I did, because they accepted her application during the highly competitive "early decision" process.

I wanted to shout for joy! But with four kids of my own to funnel through the ranks of our church, I was less interested in the whole college thing than I was in the story *behind* the story. What had spurred Cally's heart for missions? For that matter, what had spurred her heart for church? She was a regular fixture in the pews every Sunday, and she participated in pretty much everything our youth group had to offer. With a heavy academic load and a schedule bursting with such things as school sports, student government, and even a role in the high school musical, how had she managed to keep church involvement at the top of her priority list?

"My parents took us to church when we were young, and we didn't question it," Cally told me. "By the time we hit the teenage years—when we were more apt to question things— the idea of *not* going to church just wasn't an option.

"But even more than that," Cally added, "I think that I got involved in church after one of the youth leaders—a gal named Sara—reached out to me and invested her time in my life. Church groups can sometimes be sort of cliquey, and having a friend or someone to welcome you can make all the difference."

Like Cally, Eric was a bright student with an easygoing manner, a loving family, and plenty of extracurricular activities in which to be involved. Unlike Cally, though, he had little interest in going to church, and even less in getting involved in any sort of youth group or mission work. In his mind, the teens at church were a bunch of goofballs, and he wanted no part of their antics. Eric's mother, Jackie, found herself wondering where to turn for help ...

"You can't make me go back! I hate you!"

Jackie flinched at her son's words. Eric had always been a kind and courteous kid, and she had never heard him lash out at her—or anyone else—with such venom. Even so, she knew that he didn't really hate her; he was just mad because she was making him go to youth group.

Was this one of those battles that was worth fighting? Jackie wasn't sure. Reflecting on her own upbringing—she had been dropped off at the church door every week by parents who were not interested in anything "religious" but who figured that church would be a good thing for their daughter—Jackie had resolved that once she was married and had children, they would go to church *as a family*.

The first hurdle had been Jackie's husband, Peter. A sporadic churchgoer, it wasn't until he realized the influence his behavior had on his teenage son — who argued that if Dad wasn't going to church, he shouldn't have to go either — that Peter began to show up on Sunday mornings. He didn't plan to *enjoy* church; he simply went to please his wife and to set an example for his son. Somewhat to his surprise, however, he found himself hooked.

Eric, though, was another story. He didn't like church; he tolerated it because he had to. Jackie had been inspired by her Bible study teacher, a woman with five children who claimed that keeping the fourth commandment — honoring the Sabbath Day — was one of the secrets of her family's success. Citing verses like Isaiah 58:13 – 14 (which promise joy and rewards to those who honor the Sabbath by not doing whatever they please on God's holy day), the Bible study teacher said that, whether they wanted to or not, her kids knew that they had to be in church on Sunday. Jackie figured that if this woman could get *five* teens to church every week — and if it really had made a difference in their lives — then surely she could wrangle *one* teen into the pew.

And so she and Peter and Eric began attending church together as a family, and Jackie thanked God for the realization of her childhood dream. It wasn't long, though, before she caught wind of the neat things that were taking place in the church's large and vibrant youth group. The kids met on Sunday nights, and the gatherings were rumored to be filled with singing, skits, inspirational talks, and a ton of laughter. Jackie knew she was pushing it, but she decided to broach the subject with Eric.

It didn't go over well.

"What?" he said. "Now you want me to go to church in the morning *and* at night? Mom, I know what the kids at that youth group do. They do stupid stuff like throw donuts at each other. They are loud and wild—definitely not my kind of people."

"But you don't even *know* those kids!" Jackie protested.

"Exactly!" Eric agreed. "So why would I want to hang out with them?"

Undaunted, Jackie turned to the youth group leader for advice.

"Bring him for four consecutive Sundays," the man advised. "If he gets to know some of the other kids and sees what a good time we have, he will definitely want to come back."

Armed with this plan, Jackie told Eric that, like it or not, she was taking him to youth group. After the first outing, however, she lost her resolve. She knew better than to take the "I hate you" comment personally, but she didn't want to turn the whole church thing into a negative experience by starting a war over youth group. After all, Eric was going to church every Sunday. Jackie decided to be content with that.

And she decided to pray.

As much as she hated to admit it, she knew that she—the mother—was probably not in the best position to influence the thoughts and attitudes of her teenage son. Like most teens, Eric tended to view his friends' advice as far more valid and noteworthy than any counsel that his parents might toss his way. "Lord," Jackie prayed, "please open a door into Eric's heart through your Holy Spirit. Bring a friend into his life who will draw him closer to you."

It wasn't long before Jackie's prayer (a heartfelt combination of John 6:44, which says that no one comes to Jesus unless the Father draws him, and Proverbs 27:17, which addresses the stimulating effect that friends can have on one another) began to be answered. Heather was a gregarious and fun-loving girl who liked nothing more than making friends and introducing them to Jesus. For reasons that Jackie says can only be attributed to answered prayer, Heather set her sights on Eric. Captivated as he was by her enthusiasm and joy, he failed to consider the fact that she might turn out to be one of those wild donut-throwers, and when she invited him to join her at youth group, he eagerly accepted the invitation.

Jackie watched from a distance as Heather introduced Eric to other kids at church and then invited him to join the group at an overnight camp. When he asked permission to go, Jackie resisted the urge to jump up and down and shout, "Yes!" Instead, she calmly filled out the required forms and continued to pray.

At the camp, Eric surrendered his life to the Lord.

That was three years ago. Today, as Jackie tells it, the transformation in her son could not be more amazing. Not only has he participated in summer mission projects and other youth group events, but Eric has followed Heather's lead in bringing other kids to church. Stuff that once looked corny or boring is actually, Eric admits, a whole lot of fun.

"It's beyond anything I could have ever asked for," Jackie says. "I trusted God to work in Eric's life, and he has answered my prayers a hundred times beyond anything I could have ever imagined."

Looking back, Jackie acknowledges that it would have been far easier to let Eric — and, for that matter, her husband, Peter — stay home on Sundays than to prod him on toward church. But she believes that her job description as a mother includes prodding — as well as a whole lot of praying and persevering. Jackie didn't know whether it would take weeks or months or years to bring that vision to reality; what she did know was that getting her son plugged into church and into regular fellowship with other believers was something that really mattered.

"It definitely took a willingness to hang in there," Jackie says, "but it was more than worth it."

Poised for Prayer

One of the things I appreciated most about Jackie's story is that she desperately wanted her son to be involved in church, but she didn't sit in her pew comparing herself to other mothers or wondering why Eric couldn't be more like the youth group kids. She didn't worry about what she might have done *wrong*; rather, she focused on what she could do that was *right*: seeking advice from the youth pastor, keeping the lines of communication open with her son, and — most important of all — steadfastly taking her concerns to the only One who could really do anything about them.

I believe that as God looked at Jackie — and as he looks at us as we persevere in prayer — his perspective encompasses far more than anything our human eyes could ever perceive. You may *feel* like a battle-weary soldier, but God — who hears your prayers — sees you as a faithful warrior on the path to victory. You may *think* that nothing is changing, but God — who calls into being things that were not—promises to finish the good work that he has already begun.[1]

Prayer Principle

God doesn't call us parents to be successful;
he calls us to be faithful.

Whether you are waging a "prayer battle" to get your teen to church, or whether your concern is something else entirely, I want to encourage you with one of my favorite quotations from Mother Teresa. Looking around at the overwhelming tide of poverty and problems that threatened to envelop her Calcutta ministry, she never gave in to defeat or despair. "God doesn't call me to be successful," she said. "He calls me to be faithful."

Moms and Dads, that's God's call to us as well. We may want to tidy up our teens' lives with one broad wave of a magic wand, but that's not God's way. God works in the midst of people and problems—not independently of them. And his charge to us, as we wait on him to bring about all that he has promised, comes right out of Romans 12:12: "Be joyful in hope, patient in affliction, faithful in prayer."

Precious Lord, make us faithful in prayer.

---

1. Romans 4:17; Philippians 1:6.

Prayers You Can Use

Heavenly Father,

As we pray for _____'s involvement in church, help us to hold tightly to hope, knowing that you are faithful. Help us to think of ways we can encourage him toward outbursts of love and good deeds.   HEBREWS 10:23–24

Don't let _____ give up meeting together with other believers, even if some of her friends quit going to church or to youth group. Instead, help me to encourage her—and help her, in turn, to encourage others—as we look forward to your return.   HEBREWS 10:25

Let _____ be like King David, rejoicing with those who say, "Let us go to the house of the LORD."   PSALM 122:1

Remind _____ of the importance of meeting together with other believers. Show him that where two or three come together in your name, you promise to be there with them.
                    MATTHEW 18:20

Cause _____ to be devoted to the godly teaching she receives at church or in youth group, and let her place a high value on fellowship. Let her be prayerful, generous, and glad-hearted, and use her to spur on other teens in their relationship with you so that the group will grow.

ACTS 2:42–47

Teach _____ to remember the Sabbath day that you established, and to keep it holy, according to your command.

EXODUS 20:8

Help our family to understand what it means to call the Sabbath a delight and to make it an honorable day. Show us how to find our joy in you rather than in doing whatever we please. ISAIAH 58:13–14

Equip our church leaders to preach your word with great patience and careful instruction. When _____ finds herself surrounded by those who reject sound doctrine in favor of teachers who will tell them whatever their itching ears want to hear, help her to stand firm and to be able to spot the difference between truth and myths.

2 TIMOTHY 4:2–4

As _____ hears your word taught in church, may he receive the message with great eagerness and examine the Scriptures every day to see if what our minister or youth pastor is teaching is true. Don't let him be content to just sit in church; give him a holy curiosity to read the Bible for himself.   ACTS 17:11

Prompt _____ to be like Lydia, who listened to the apostles teach on the Sabbath. Open _____'s heart so that she will respond to your message and want to be with other believers.   ACTS 16:13–14

Let _____ enjoy the company of people who are "salty"—those whose presence creates a thirst for Jesus. Help _____ and the other teens in our church to live at peace with each other.   MARK 9:50

Give _____ the same Spirit that Jesus had as a young man. Let him be an eager listener and an active participant at church, and bless him with wisdom and understanding.
          LUKE 2:46–47

CHAPTER 10

Praying for
Dating Relationships

Walk with the wise and become wise;
associate with fools and get in trouble.
PROVERBS 13:20 NLT

I just now grabbed a copy of *Praying the Scriptures for Your Children* from my bookshelf. Not wanting to repeat myself, I was eager to see what I had written about dating relationships in the earlier book. Much to my surprise and — I'll admit it — chagrin, I found that I hadn't written anything. Not even a paragraph! There's a chapter on praying for your child's friendships, and another one about marriage — but what about all those in-between years, the ones where your son's hormones are raging and your daughter flips for the guy with the tattoo and the Mohawk? *What was I thinking*, neglecting an entire prayer season like that?

Looking back, I realized that Hillary — the oldest of our four children — had just celebrated her tenth birthday when I shipped the first *Praying the Scriptures* manuscript to the folks at Zondervan. At a time when we spent most nights memorizing math facts and tucked the children into bed at about the time the sun went down, things like dating and curfews were not even on my radar screen. I remember working on an article about courtship for *Focus on the Family* magazine. Courtship, an alternative to traditional dating, allows a guy who is serious about a girl (serious enough to be thinking about eventual marriage) to spend time "courting" her (in the presence of family members or trusted friends), so that he can determine whether or not she is "the one" (and so that she and her family can eyeball him at the same time). I found the subject worthwhile, intriguing, and — since Hillary had a third grade diorama project on *Stuart Little* due the same week — entirely forgettable. After all, we had *years* to go before we had to figure out all that boyfriend-girlfriend stuff.

That was then. This is now. And with three girls currently "of age" on the dating scene (Virginia, as a seventh grader, insisted that she was the only kid she knew who was not allowed to "go out" with anyone), I am more than interested in the subject, both in praying for my kids and in culling advice from older friends who have made it through this season and whose children are now walking the marriage aisle with their purity — and their hearts — intact.

"We were committed to the idea of courtship, so we did not allow our children to date," one mother told me. "It wasn't easy. I remember standing next to the vegetables in our grocery store while a woman I knew screamed at me, telling me that we were crazy and that everyone was talking about how weird we were."

"We allowed our kids to date, but we had some rules," another friend confided. "One was that they couldn't be at anyone's house if the parents weren't home. I remember dropping our daughter off at a boy's house and then, when we noticed there weren't any cars in the driveway, going back to ring the doorbell. The fellow assured us that his folks would be 'right back.' We waited—somewhat to our daughter's mortification—but they never showed up. The boy had lied to our daughter, knowing that she would never have come over had she known that his parents were gone."

"When our children were teens," a third mom said, "they hung out a lot in groups. When their friends began pairing off, we prayed for a hedge of protection to be put around their emotions so that they would not be drawn to anyone whom God didn't want them to be with. I remember not liking my son's girlfriend very much when he first brought her home. By the time they got engaged, however, I found myself grateful that God had done the picking and not me—she is absolutely perfect for my son."

Suffice it to say that within the realm of Christian parenting there is a *huge* spectrum of perspectives, practices, and even prayers about dating. I have a good friend who is always looking for a set of rules or a formula for godly living—"Just tell me how to do it, God, and I will," she says—and I'm afraid she is going to hate this chapter. The more parents I talk with, the more convinced I am that teenage dating is one of those areas where, as soon as you think you have a workable system, God tosses you a parenting curveball.

My friend Teri, for example, is a homeschooling former missionary who has done pretty much everything right. She'd be lightning-quick to counter that claim, but from where I sit, her kids look fairly fantastic. They are athletic, smart, respectful, kind, and—best of all—absolutely in love with Jesus. But when her oldest daughter developed more than a passing interest in a boy she had met at church, Teri and her husband, Bart, knew it was a relationship that could rock their world ...

***

"But, Mom, I really like him! Justin is an amazing guy. You and Daddy *have* to let me go out with him—please!"

Teri listened to Wendy's impassioned plea and wondered if she could be dreaming. If she had the right boy—and she knew that she did—she couldn't see any possible way that her daughter could be attracted to him. Wendy was a rule-follower, a straight-A student, and an incredibly talented and hardworking athlete. Justin was an overweight pothead who had recently been kicked out of school.

Well, OK, maybe he wasn't technically a pothead. But Justin *had* smoked the stuff—everyone knew that—and that, coupled with a long history of disrespect for teachers and a blowout night of binge drinking, had resulted in his expulsion from the Christian school that Teri and Bart's older children attended. Teri was as willing to extend grace as the next person, but as she reflected on the chaos that Justin had reportedly caused in the classes he shared with Wendy's sister, Samantha, she had to admit that she didn't blame the school for asking him to leave. No doubt about it—the boy was Trouble, with a capital *T.*

The irony of it all, Teri realized, was that Wendy hadn't even noticed Justin at school. They had kindled a friendship in the Dominican Republic, on a mission trip sponsored by their church. A mission trip! How did a kid like Justin even get to *go* on a mission trip?

If that was God's way of being funny, Teri wasn't laughing.

Truth be told, Teri knew why Justin had been part of the mission team. The expulsion had served as a wake-up call of sorts, and Justin had recommitted his life to the Lord. He began showing up at church and youth group events with amazing regularity, and—over the protests of a few adults in the church who saw him as a dangerous influence on their teens—one of the youth directors had accepted his application for the team. "He's ready," the director had said, putting an end to the discussion.

Teri agreed that Justin was ready—she just wasn't sure for what. With his long hair, baggy clothes, and six-foot seven-inch-anything-but-lanky frame, Justin looked more apt to serve time than he did to serve God. When she and Bart had taught Wendy to pay more attention to someone's heart than to his outward appearance, Teri never dreamed that her daughter would take them *that* seriously.

"OK," she found herself saying in response to Wendy's request. "You and Justin can spend time together. But you can't be alone. You can see him at youth group, or if a group of kids goes out to lunch after church."

Wondering how long the attraction would last, Teri and Bart decided to pull their youth pastor into the discussion. "We want you to know what's going on between Wendy and Justin," they confided. "We're not very comfortable with their relationship, and we'd be grateful if you could keep an eye on them while they're at church."

"All right," the pastor said, "but there's something you should know. When we were in the Dominican Republic, nobody—and I mean nobody—worked harder or demonstrated as much integrity as Justin."

Somewhat mollified, Teri and Bart kept any further reservations to themselves, confident that Wendy would lose interest in Justin soon enough. If nothing else, the fact that college was just around the corner would shake things loose. Wendy was a rising senior with the grades and other achievements she needed to get into a Top-25 school, and she had expressed interest in a string of colleges dotting the Eastern seaboard.

A couple of months passed, and Wendy's attachment to Justin looked stronger than ever. The only thing that had changed, it seemed, were the geographic boundaries she put on her college search. "I'm thinking of going someplace closer to home, maybe an hour or so away," she said—leaving no doubt about her plans to put as little distance as possible between herself and her man.

Things finally came to a head one afternoon when Teri and Wendy were home alone. "Can Justin and I go out for dinner tonight?" Wendy asked.

"Sure—as long as you're with a group of kids," Teri said, reciting the guidelines she and Bart had placed on the time that the couple spent together.

"Mom!" Wendy cried. "Why are you and Daddy making this so hard? If I were dating some other guy from church—somebody who could talk the talk and who looked the look—it wouldn't be any problem for us to be together! You're not being fair!"

"Wendy," Teri said, struggling to keep the emotion out of her voice, "it all has to do with Justin's track record. I know he seems like a great guy to you, but it's only been a couple of months since he was making some pretty bad choices. You are our daughter, and we love you. We just need you to be careful."

"I'll be in college next year!" Wendy wailed. "You have to start giving me my freedom!"

"I know, and we will."

"When?" Wendy demanded angrily. "How much longer are you and Daddy going to try to keep us apart?"

"I can't give you an answer on that right now," Teri sighed. "We just need you to trust us." Being a natural peacemaker, she hated the way the conversation was going. Wendy could be very stubborn, and it was clear that nothing Teri could say would calm her down. Teri decided to go downstairs before saying something she might regret.

"Lord," she prayed, "You are the only one who can work this out. Bart and I believe that we need to stand firm on this one. I thought I could bring Wendy around and help her understand that all we're trying to do is to love her and protect her, but I can't do it. We need you, Lord."

An hour later, Teri went back upstairs, intending to check on Wendy to see if she was OK. She pushed open her bedroom door, expecting a stony reception, and was more than a little surprised when Wendy bounded across the room.

"You're not going to believe what happened!" Wendy said, wrapping her arms around her mother.

"Tell me!" Teri gasped.

"After you left my room, I called Justin. He said I had really messed up, and that it was my job to respect you and Daddy. I hung up the phone and decided to read my Bible and pray.

I felt like God was telling me I had a choice to make. I could trust him and obey you—or not. I decided I should obey you."

"You did?" Teri could hardly believe her ears.

"Yes—but Mom, that's not the best part. When we were arguing earlier, I thought my life was *over*. But once I made the decision to obey you, I found myself just filled up with joy! It's amazing!"

Yes, Teri agreed—teenage dramatics notwithstanding—it really was amazing. *God* was amazing. All that Teri had been hoping—praying—for was a little peace between herself and her strong-willed daughter, and God had done so much more. It was the fulfillment of Jesus' promise in John 15: "When you obey me,... you will be filled with my joy. Yes, your joy will overflow!"[1]

Not only had God brought peace and joy into their home, but, Teri realized, he had answered a prayer that she and Bart had been praying over the teens' relationship. They had been asking God to help Wendy and Justin sharpen one another, according to Proverbs 27:17. Embarrassed as she was to admit it, Teri acknowledged that she had been counting on Wendy to "sharpen" Justin's spiritual life—but she hadn't really expected the prayer to work in reverse.

Reflecting on God's goodness, Teri and Bart sensed that something had changed. They still didn't want the kids spending time together alone, and they weren't about to let Wendy turn her back on some of the colleges that had piqued her interest in the pre-Justin days, but the door had been opened a crack, and the light was coming in.

---

1. John 15:10–11 NLT.

God had used Justin — with his checkered past and his grungy-looking present — to show them a little slice of his glory.

Prayer Principle

Trust God to do the things you can't — and look for
him to show up in ways you don't expect.

Poised for Prayer

I mentioned earlier that perspectives and practices on teen-age dating vary widely among families. Maybe that's because the Bible doesn't give us a whole lot of commands or specific information on the subject. There are plenty of principles and proverbs — things like "guard your heart" and "do not be yoked together with unbelievers"[1] — but rarely do we find hard-and-fast rules couched in language such as, "Be home by eleven o'clock."

That being said, the Bible does offer some relevant verses to support some of the commonsense advice I picked up while researching this chapter. Here are some examples (advice followed by Scripture):

- Make sure your teen has a predetermined escape plan, just in case he or she needs to get out of an uncomfortable or potentially dangerous situation. One fitting reference is 2 Timothy 2:22, which urges believers to "flee the evil desires of youth."

---

1. Proverbs 4:23; 2 Corinthians 6:14.

- Remind your teen — and your teen's date — of the importance of honor. A guy needs to treat a girl the way he hopes some other fella is treating his future wife. Or as Romans 12:10 says, "Be devoted to one another in brotherly love. Honor one another above yourselves."

- Set boundaries for things like physical intimacy, and be specific. There's a lot more to maintaining pure hearts, minds, and bodies than just not having sex. Song of Songs 2:7 cautions against prematurely arousing or awakening feelings of love, and 1 Thessalonians 4:3–5 is even more blunt: "It is God's will that ... each of you should learn to control his own body in a way that is holy and honorable, not in passionate lust like the heathens, who do not know God."

- Encourage group dating. One-on-one, unsupervised dating raises both temptations and questions. The King James Version's rendering of 1 Thessalonians 5:22 exhorts us to avoid even the "*appearance* of evil" — and if I'm going to start putting things in italics, I might as well throw in Ephesians 5:3: "Among you there must not be even a *hint* of sexual immorality."

- Evaluate dating relationships based on how time spent together affects the teens' attitudes and behavior. What we want to see is the fulfillment of verses such as Hebrews 10:24: "Let us consider how we may spur one another on toward love and good deeds."

These are, of course, just a handful of practical pointers — and I'm sure that, if we put our parenting heads together, we could come up with a whole bookful of similar nuggets. At the end of the day, though, even my formula-loving friend would agree that what we really want isn't a set of rules. What we want—for ourselves and for our teens—is a *relationship*: a hope-infusing, wisdom-giving, life-changing relationship with the Lord himself. As we pray for our kids, asking for things such as wisdom and protection in their dating relationships, let's also ask God to draw them to himself, filling their hearts and minds with a love that is deeper and richer than anything they could ever imagine.

Prayers You Can Use

Heavenly Father,

Let _____ be drawn to girls and relationships who will sharpen him spiritually and mentally. Let him, likewise, seek always to bring out the best in the girls he spends time with.   PROVERBS 27:17

As _____ begins forging relationships with young men, help her to guard her heart, knowing that it will affect everything she does.   PROVERBS 4:23

Remind _____ of your counsel, that we should not be "yoked together" with those who do not know you. Let him take the question "What does a believer have in common with an unbeliever?" very seriously, and prompt him to seek out common ground with other believers.

2 CORINTHIANS 6:14–15

Set a hedge of protection around _____, that she might be protected from harm and drawn only to the young man whom you would choose to be her companion.   JOB 1:10

Let _____'s love be sincere. Cause him to hate what is evil in your sight and to cling to that which is good. Let him be devoted to his girlfriend with brotherly love, honoring her above himself.   ROMANS 12:9–10

When _____ finds herself having to choose between obedience to you and going her own way, help her to choose obedience—and as she does, let her heart be filled with overflowing joy.   JOHN 15:10–11

As _____ considers the girls he wants to spend time with, let him submit to your authority so that your peace can rule in his heart, causing him to know exactly what he should say or do and whether or not his interest in a particular girl is pleasing to you.   COLOSSIANS 3:15

As _____ spends time with young men, let her be careful and watch herself closely so that she does not forget your commands or let them slip from her heart. Remind her of the things we have taught her about your laws and your love.   DEUTERONOMY 4:9

Cause _____'s love to abound more and more in knowledge and depth of insight, so that he may be able to discern what is best and may be pure and blameless until the day of Christ.   PHILIPPIANS 1:9–10

Equip _____ to flee from sexual immorality, recognizing that her body is a temple of the Holy Spirit. Remind her that she belongs to you and that she is to honor you with her body.   1 CORINTHIANS 6:18–20

When _____ finds himself yearning for a dating relationship, help him to stay watchful and prayerful so that he will not fall into temptation. Let him be strong and take heart as he waits on your perfect provision.

MATTHEW 26:41; PSALM 27:14

Be faithful, Lord, and do not let _____ be tempted beyond what she can bear. When she is tempted, provide a way out so that she can stand up under it.

1 CORINTHIANS 10:13

As we establish rules and boundaries for dating in our home, give us wisdom and knowledge, so that we may properly lead our teens, for they are precious in your sight, and they belong to you.   2 CHRONICLES 1:10

CHAPTER 11

Praying for Your Teen's Relationship with Christ

So then, just as you received Christ Jesus as Lord,
continue to live in him, rooted and built up in him, strengthened in
the faith as you were taught, and overflowing with thankfulness.
COLOSSIANS 2:6–7

After dropping our combined eight children off on the first day of school, my friend Anne and I decided to stop for a cup of coffee. We headed to Starbucks, where we were delighted to run into Kathy, a friend I hadn't seen in years.

"How old are your kids now?" Kathy asked.

When she learned that Anne and I had four teens between us, Kathy broke into a huge smile. "I remember those days!" she cried. "And I want you to meet my friend Patty. Patty's son is married to my daughter."

Kathy pulled Patty into our circle, and the four of us stood there, holding our coffee cups and swapping stories. "Patty and I have been friends forever," Kathy said. "Our kids grew up together in Chicago, and even after we moved east, we stayed in touch."

"Remember when we took that vacation to St. Simon's Island?" Patty prompted.

"Oh, yes!" Kathy said. "Our kids were teens—and you can imagine the kinds of things that were weighing on our hearts. Patty and I snuck off one day and found this little chapel where we could pray. We spent the entire morning just pouring out our hearts to the Lord, like it says in Lamentations 2:19, lifting up our hands to him for the lives of our children."

"We prayed for each one of them by name, one at a time—" Patty added.

"—and we never dreamed that two of them would grow up and get married to each other!" Kathy finished.

As Kathy and Patty continued to reminisce, Anne and I exchanged a look. I knew what she was thinking: we needed to get away and take some serious time to pray for our kids, one by one.

"Let's do it tomorrow," Anne suggested.

The next day, we met at the beach, right next to the big wooden Cape Henry cross that marks the spot where the Jamestown colonists first landed. We poured out our hearts, and then—just as we finished—the sky poured down rain. We snatched up our prayer journals and bolted for the car.

"We need to do this again!" Anne said, laughing.

"Yes," I agreed, "just as soon as my Bible dries out."

I am so grateful to God that he allowed us to run into Kathy and Patty. Their friendship, their parenting testimony, and their prayers were such an inspiration—and that first-day-of-school cup of coffee didn't hurt either. Go fix yourself a cup, if you like, because I want to invite you into our circle and then share one of Kathy's stories with you ...

Kathy and Steve loved the fact that their kids were friends with all sorts of people. Rather than hang out in any particular clique or group at school, their son Carl enjoyed being with the preps, the church kids, the skaters, and—perhaps most of all—the athletes. As a six-year-old boy, Carl had met—and, much to his delight, actually *touched*—his idol, Michael Jordan, and his greatest dream was to follow in this basketball player's footsteps.

By the time Carl hit high school, it looked as though his dream might come true. A star player on the school's basketball team, he set his sights on playing Division I ball. In addition to his athletic talent, he seemed to have everything that a teenage boy could wish for: a cute girlfriend, a whole pack of guys to run around with, and parents who truly loved him.

In Steve and Kathy's mind, though, something was missing. Carl had been raised in the church, and at the age of five, he had asked to be baptized. Once he got his driver's license, he worked his way around town to all the various neighborhoods, picking up kids and bringing them to a nondenominational youth group, where a number of teens had come to faith in Christ. Deep down, though, Kathy knew that her son was not walking with the Lord. Basketball was the only thing he really cared about.

"Make him a man," Steve prayed day in and day out. "Make him a man of God."

Listening to her husband pray, Kathy wished that she shared his optimism. She truly wanted to believe that her son would become a man of God, but—looking at his friends (many of his peers were making some seriously bad choices) and his total lack of interest in anything remotely connected to church (except for the socially oriented youth group) — she just didn't see how it could happen. And when Carl graduated from high school and got a job busing tables at a local nightclub, Kathy worried that he'd slip even further away.

"He can't work in that horrible place!" she said to Steve. "You've got to do something!"

"He got a summer job, just like we asked him to. Don't worry," Steve said. "He'll be fine."

One night, some of Kathy and Steve's friends — a family in town for the weekend — decided to visit the nightclub. "Let's go say hi to Carl at work," one of the college-aged visitors suggested. "We can dance — it'll be fun!"

The group trooped off to the night spot — only to find it closed for the evening, with no sign of Carl. Kathy tried to hide her concern from their guests, but when Carl still had not returned by three in the morning — four hours after his curfew — she was frantic.

Once again, Steve provided a calming presence. "He'll be back," he said.

Carl did come back — and found himself facing his father's wrath. "You need to stay by my side for the rest of the weekend so that you can be with our guests. After that, you're moving out."

"What?" Carl asked.

"You heard me. You can't live in our house if you're going to show such total disregard for our rules. You're heading off to college in six weeks. I'm sure you'll find someplace to live until then."

Carl moved into an apartment with a couple of guys. Had Kathy known what he was eating — leftover scraps from the tables he bused — she might have worried even more than she initially did, but she understood the importance of being united with her husband, and she knew that making her son face the consequences of his actions was, in the end, the right thing to do.

Carl hit the college campus without his hoped-for basketball scholarship, but he managed to land a spot on the team as a walk-on. Meanwhile, Kathy continued to pray for her son's relationship with the Lord. She would go into his empty bedroom, put her hands on his bed, and cry out to God. "Let Carl know how much you love him," she prayed. "Let him grasp how wide and long and high and deep your love is — and cause him to surrender his life to you."[1]

Prayer Principle

Pray in your teen's bedroom when he is not home.
Play Christian music and invite
the Holy Spirit to take up residence there.

She also sent care packages to Carl's dorm — stacks and stacks of Christian music CDs that she hoped he would listen to. If nothing else, she knew that the CDs would make him at least *think* about the Lord — and serve as a reminder that his mother was praying.

Carl's first year at school passed without incident. He loved playing basketball, and he seemed to get along well with the other players. During the fall of his second year, however, Carl called home, and Kathy could tell that he was upset.

---

1. Ephesians 3:18.

"You're playing basketball at a Division I school, right?" Kathy asked.

"Right."

"And you're dating a beautiful girl?"

"Right."

"And you're not all that happy."

"Right."

"Well," Kathy sighed, "I don't know what else to say, other than what Daddy and I have always told you. Until you really surrender your life to the Lord, you will never find the peace and the joy that you're looking for."

Carl didn't say much, and so Kathy continued. "I love you, son. You know I do. But this is a decision you need to make for yourself; I cannot do it for you."

She hung up the telephone, thinking that she'd said the same thing to Carl — that he needed to give his life completely to Jesus — a hundred times before. Maybe this time he'd listen.

For reasons that even Carl does not fully understand, that phone call — and the calm assurance in his mother's voice — served as a turning point in his life. And as he looked around and saw several top athletes getting drunk every night, with nothing to show for it, he realized that the life of a basketball star — at least one who wasn't walking with the Lord — was not one that he wanted.

Carl decided to transfer to a college closer to home. It wasn't a Division I school, but he could still play basketball, and he figured that a change of scenery might help settle his restless heart. Still, though, he wasn't ready to turn his life over to God. He moved in with his parents — but things like getting up early on Sunday morning to go to church with them were definitely *not* in his plans.

"You can't *make* me go," Carl said, stubbornly. "I'm in college now, and I'm an adult. I want to live my own life."

Steve's tough love showed its face again. "You can live your own life when you can pay your own way. If you want to live here, you have to go to church. I don't care if you lie down on the floor in the back and go to sleep. You *need* to go with us on Sunday."

Grudgingly, Carl started going to church. He didn't say much about the music or the sermons, and Kathy and Steve were content to keep praying.

One Sunday, when Steve was out of town on business, it was Kathy's turn to pray with people during the altar call. When the pastor invited people to come forward if they wanted to give their lives to the Lord, she saw a familiar figure walk down the aisle.

It was Carl.

Poised for Prayer

Carl surrendered his life to the Lord that day. He went on to graduate school at a Bible college, got married, and came back to Kathy and Steve's church to head up the young adult ministry. The group was about sixty people strong when he arrived; today, more than six hundred folks, aged eighteen to thirty-five, pack the worship hall each week to hear Carl preach.

"There were so many things that Steve and I did wrong," Kathy says, "but we hung in there with Carl and kept pointing him toward the Lord.

"I know that you can't force a relationship with God on your children, but you can try to get them in an atmosphere — such as in a Bible-believing church — where their hearts and their eyes might be opened. The Bible says that God's word will not return empty or void,[1] and Carl is a living testimony to that truth and to God's amazing grace.

"I would never have believed it," she admits, "but our son has become — just like his daddy prayed — a man of God."

For his part, Carl is equally aware of God's work in his life. He has shared his testimony from the pulpit, and when parents come to him for advice — as they often do — he encourages them to follow Kathy and Steve's example. "I laughed when my mom mailed me all of those Christian CDs," he says, "and I threw them away. I didn't like all their rules or the consequences I had to face. But through it all, I knew that my parents loved me and that they were always praying."

Let's love our kids, too, and let's never stop praying — no matter how far our teens wander or how long it takes to bring them back.

Lord, make them into men — and women — of God.

---

1. Isaiah 55:11.

Prayers You Can Use

Heavenly Father,

Let _____ remember his Creator in the days of his youth.   ECCLESIASTES 12:1

Tune _____'s ears to hear your voice so that, as Samuel did when he was a boy, she will invite you to speak to her and then will listen to your words.   1 SAMUEL 3:9 – 10

Allow _____ to be rooted and established in love. Give him power to grasp how wide and long and high and deep your love is. Let him know this love that surpasses all understanding, that he may be completely filled with your grace.

EPHESIANS 3:18 – 19

Cause _____ to put her trust in you and never be shaken.   PSALM 125:1

Give _____ a singleness of heart and put a new spirit within him. Take away his heart of stone and give him a tender heart instead, so that he will obey you. Let him know that he belongs to you.   EZEKIEL 11:19 – 20

Remove any trace of a veil from _____'s eyes. Take the blinders off of her mind—wherever she is prone to unbelief—so that she might understand the gospel and see the light of your glory.   2 CORINTHIANS 4:3–6

Prompt _____ to confess with his mouth that Jesus is Lord. Let him believe in his heart that you have raised Jesus from the dead. Let him call on your name and be saved.

ROMANS 10:9, 13

When Satan wants to sift _____ like wheat, I pray—along with you, Lord Jesus—that her faith may not fail. And when she turns back to you, equip her to strengthen others.   LUKE 22:31–32

Do not let _____ be stiff-necked; instead, cause him to submit to you. Let him return to you so that you can pour out your compassion and your grace on his life.

2 CHRONICLES 30:8–9

Put people in _____'s life who will gently teach her. Change her heart wherever it needs changing, so that she will believe the truth.   2 TIMOTHY 2:25

Open _____'s eyes and turn him from darkness to light, and from the power of Satan to you, so that he may receive forgiveness of his sins and a place among those who are sanctified by faith in Christ.   ACTS 26:18

Teach _____ to pray, just as Jesus taught the disciples. Let her depend on you for her daily bread, for forgiveness, and for protection from temptation.   LUKE 11:1–4

Bring my teen back to the faith that he knew as a child. Let our mouths be filled with laughter, and our tongues with songs of joy. Let our friends and neighbors know that you have done great things for our family.   PSALM 126:1–2

PART 3

PRAYING
for Your **TEEN'S**
HEALTH
and SAFETY

CHAPTER 12

Praying for
Your Teenage Driver

*He will command his angels concerning you
to guard you in all your ways.*
PSALM 91:11

When our daughter Hillary got her driver's license, one of her friends—who had himself clipped a mailbox early on in his driving career—said he'd give her twenty bucks if she could go a whole month without hitting anything. I quickly realized that my parental admonitions to "be careful!" were nothing compared to the satisfaction Hillary would get out of looting her friend, and when the first month passed without incident, I thought about slipping the guy another twenty to see if he could get her to go double or nothing.

Teens and cars—like teens and almost anything that runs on gas or electricity—can be an unsettling mix. Sometimes the end result is aggravating, like the burn mark on the bathroom counter from the hair straightener that was left on all day, or the broken window that failed to survive the rocket-launcher science project. Sometimes it's a little bit funny, like the time one of my husband's relatives tried to unclog a toilet by using a cherry bomb (don't try it), or the time my girlfriend's daughter closed her eyes while piloting a motor scooter so that she could "feel the breeze in her face and the wind in her hair" — and wound up feeling a mailbox. And sometimes it turns into a parent's worst nightmare. I'm not the weepy sort, but I still can't hear my friend Anne tell her story without reaching for the Kleenex ...

Anne grabbed a half-finished Gatorade and shoved the bottle into the trash bag she was holding. With all four of her children involved in multiple sports, she sometimes felt like her car was a locker room. She pulled a sock out from under one of the seats, grateful for a sunny day and a moment's peace so that she could get herself organized for the week ahead.

Fifteen minutes earlier, Anne had waved good-bye to her husband, Bob, and their oldest daughter, fifteen-year-old Peyton. Peyton had been driving with a learner's permit for a month, and when Bob said that he wanted to catch up on some work at his office, Peyton had offered to drive him there. The twenty-five-minute ride to and from the office would allow her to log some highway miles, and she figured that she could use the weekend's quiet to study while her dad worked.

Anne could hear her seven-year-old son, Robert, playing basketball with a friend. Suddenly, another sound pierced the air: it was her cell phone, which she had — providentially — brought outside while she worked.

"Hello?" she said, cradling the phone under one ear.

The voice on the other end was incoherent. It sounded like Peyton, but Anne couldn't make out her words. Whatever it was, something was terribly wrong.

"Peyton—calm down!" Anne cried, her heart pounding. "Tell me what's wrong!"

Peyton continued to scream, her words coming fast and on top of each other. A few words suddenly cut through the jumble: *"I killed Daddy! I killed Daddy!"*

Anne's vision blurred. She knew she was going to faint. And then, in an instant, she felt calm and detached—like this horrible drama was unfolding in another world, happening to someone she did not know.

"Peyton, please calm down," Anne repeated. "Catch your breath."

It was as though her daughter had not heard. Peyton continued to wail. Finally another voice came on the phone—one that Anne did not recognize. "Your husband and your daughter have been in an accident," the woman said. "Your daughter is fine, and the rescue workers are with your husband right now."

Adrenaline took over. Hardly knowing what she was doing, Anne grabbed Robert and his friend, pushed them into the car, and began driving. "Jesus, save my husband!" she cried, over and over again. "Please, Jesus! Save him!"

When she reached the highway, all of the lanes were clogged. Seeing rescue lights in the distance, Anne steered her car into the emergency lane and sped forward. She got as close as she could, and then, telling the boys to stay put, she jumped out of the car. A fireman approached.

"Tell me the truth!" Anne begged. "What happened to my husband?"

"He's alive," the man said, "but they're taking him to the hospital. The car flipped three times."

Anne's eyes searched the scene. She saw the ambulance, and then her white Suburban, its top crushed nearly flat and its windows completely gone. No one, she thought, could have survived. Suddenly, Peyton was there, crying hysterically.

"I'm so sorry, Mom. I'm so sorry!"

Anne hugged her daughter tightly and then released her into the arms of a stranger. She had to find Bob. Hurrying toward the ambulance, she could see a stretcher inside. She pushed past the crowd of medical workers and threw herself onto her husband. *"Please, Jesus! Please ..."*

I met up with Anne later that day at the hospital. Bob was still in the emergency room. He had suffered a slight concussion, and the doctors were busy taking glass shards out of his head. Apart from that, he was fine. And aside from a few cuts on her legs, Peyton was unharmed as well.

"It's a miracle!" Anne said. "It's a miracle that they crossed three lanes of highway traffic and didn't hit any other cars. It's a miracle that they're alive! The man who pulled Peyton out of the car asked her if she believed in angels. He saw the whole thing happen — and he said that angels had saved her. I believe it."

I believed it too — particularly after Anne shared one of her favorite prayer verses with me. "Psalm 91," she said. "Especially verses 11 and 12, where it says that God will give his angels charge over you, to keep you in all your ways and bear you up, lest you dash your foot against a stone. I pray these verses pretty much every day for my family."

Psalm 91 ends with God's promise that when we acknowledge his name, we can call on him and know that he will protect us and answer us. He promises to be with us — and our children — in times of trouble and to deliver us (verses 14 and 15).

I remember speaking to a congregation in the San Francisco area, where I had been asked to give a message on the power of praying the Scriptures. Afterward, an older gentleman approached. His eyes were bright blue, and they glistened with tears. "I was a teen when I served in World War II," he told me. "When I came home, my father showed me Psalm 91. He said he had prayed it for me every single day while I was gone."

That's how it is with God's Word. A psalm that was written three thousand years ago is just as powerful and applicable today as it was over sixty years ago, when a young soldier fought in Europe, and as it was three years ago, when a young driver was on the highway. The promises and provision that David recognized when he wrote Psalm 91 are the very same promises and provision that we can count on in this very moment. As Isaiah 40:8 puts it, "The grass withers and the flowers fall, but the word of our God stands forever."

Prayer Principle

God doesn't change. Neither does his Word.
When you pray the Scriptures,
you tap into the same power that has been working
in the lives of teens forever.

Poised for Prayer

In the same way, God himself does not change. James 1:17 says that every "good and perfect gift is from above, coming down from the Father of the heavenly lights, who does not change like shifting shadows." Safety and protection are gifts that all of us want for our children. When we ask God to give these gifts to our kids—whether they're in the car or anyplace else—we can do so knowing that he has a long history of keeping his eye on teens. He shut the lions' mouths for Daniel and shielded his friends from the scorching flames of the fiery furnace. He rescued a young Queen Esther from the genocidal schemes of her vile adversary. And he protected David, the boy armed only with a slingshot and a handful of stones, from the power and wrath of a giant.[1]

Sometimes I wish that the Bible gave us more insight into how the *parents* of some of these teens felt. When David's dad sent him to the battlefield, it was with instructions to bring some bread and cheese to his older brothers and to report back on how they were faring against the Philistines. I suspect he had no idea that the boy would drop off the meal and then decide to take on a giant! But isn't that always the way it is? Who can predict what a teen will do?

The teen years show us, as perhaps never before, that our parental influence is limited. We are no longer in control. We cannot always be with our kids, and we don't always know whom they are with—a lot of times, we aren't even sure where, exactly, they are. We can't be there to tell our teens how fast to drive, where to turn, or even what to say or do in any given situation (and even if we could do these things, would they listen?). We can warn them, encourage them, teach them, and even threaten them—but at the end of the day, they are out of our reach.

---

1. See Daniel 6; 1 Samuel 17; Esther 3–8.

But they are *never* out of God's reach. His arm, as he reminds us repeatedly, is never too short.[1]

And not only that, but when our kids come up against a rocky place—whether a sickness, an accident, or the consequence of a foolish decision (like putting a cherry bomb in a toilet)—God promises to be with them. I love how he puts it in Isaiah 43:2 (NLT): "When you go through deep waters and great trouble, I will be with you. When you go through rivers of difficulty, you will not drown! When you walk through the fire of oppression, you will not be burned up; the flames will not consume you."

Note that this verse does not say *if* you go through deep waters, but *when*. Trouble and difficulty and fiery trials are sure to come—and sometimes the teen years are where we find the deepest waters and the hottest fires. Our faith will be tested. But as we turn our kids over to the Lord, trusting in his long arm and his mighty presence, we can be confident that, ultimately, he *will* bring them through.

---

1. Numbers 11:23; Isaiah 59:1.

Prayers You Can Use

Heavenly Father,

When _____ gets behind the wheel, guide him in the way of wisdom and lead him along straight paths.

PROVERBS 4:11

As _____ drives, keep her in perfect peace. Make her way smooth, and let her follow your laws — including things like speed limits!

ISAIAH 26:3 – 8

When disaster strikes [in the form of a flat tire, an accident, or some other mishap], send your angels to encamp around _____ and minister to him with your comfort, protection, and healing.

PSALM 34:7; HEBREWS 1:14

Help me release _____ to you when she gets behind the wheel or in the car with her friends, knowing that as I cast all my anxiety on you, you will care for my daughter — and for me.

1 PETER 5:7

Watch over _____ so that his foot will not slip. By day and by night, protect him from all harm along the roads. Watch over his life as he comes and goes.

PSALM 121:3 – 8

When _____ faces difficulty on the road [getting lost, traffic jams, and so on], don't let her become frightened or dismayed. Remind her that you are with her and that you will strengthen her and help her.   ISAIAH 41:10

Stand at _____'s side and give him strength. Even as you delivered Daniel from the lions' den, please rescue _____ from every evil attack and danger, and bring him safely to your heavenly kingdom.   2 TIMOTHY 4:17–18

Give _____ victory and be her shield. Guard her course and protect her way.   PROVERBS 2:7–8

Don't let _____ drive like Jehu—like a madman— and don't let him cast off restraint. Instead, prompt him to keep the law so that he will be blessed.

    2 KINGS 9:20; PROVERBS 29:18

Protect _____ so that she will not be an anxious driver. Let her be self-controlled and alert to danger.

    1 PETER 5:7–8

As _____ gets behind the wheel, keep him from being wise in his own eyes. Give him a healthy level of fear, and let him exercise sound judgment and discernment.

    PROVERBS 3:7, 21

CHAPTER 13

Praying for Your Teenage Athlete

Everyone who competes in the games goes into strict training.
They do it to get a crown that will not last;
but we do it to get a crown that will last forever.

1 CORINTHIANS 9:25

Many of my prayer partners have children who play sports. While the giftedness of each individual athlete varies widely — we've prayed for state champions as well as for perennial bench-warmers — we moms share many common concerns.

We want our kids to be men and women of character: Half the reason I signed my kids up for soccer when they were barely out of diapers was that I'd heard that sports develop things like self-discipline, perseverance, and a willingness to sacrifice your own interests for the good of a team.

We want our kids to grow up healthy and strong. One of my friends reported that, after listening to her pray one day, her son said, "Mom, as long as you're praying that I will get to be five foot ten, why don't you just go ahead and make it six feet?"

And perhaps more than anything — at least from the vantage point of the sidelines during the heat of competition — we want our kids to be safe. Robbie was only ten years old when he started coming out of football and lacrosse games with more bruises than a late-season peach, and I realized—duh!—that he really could get hurt out there. Shoulder pads were fine, but I didn't want him to take the field unless he'd also been covered in prayer!

Psalm 121:3 promises that the God who watches over us will "neither slumber nor sleep." He is always on watch. And unlike the parents who sit beside me in the stands, God never misses one of the plays. His view is unobstructed, his attention is focused, and—as Jesus reminds us in Matthew 6:8—he knows exactly what our teens need, even before we ask him.

My friend Kenzie is raising two very athletic boys. Her son Trey began winning road races in elementary school, crossing the finish line with enough time to suck down a Gatorade before the next challenger even came into view. When I talked to Kenzie a couple of weeks ago, Trey had just landed a spot on the track team at the University of Virginia.

For Kenzie's other son, Duncan, the athletic road hasn't been quite as smooth. Like all the praying moms I know, Kenzie routinely asks God to protect her kids—but what she has discovered is that God's idea of keeping a teen safe sometimes comes with unexpected twists and turns ...

By the time Duncan was in middle school, it was obvious that he was going to be a big guy. He shot past his mom, his dad, and his older brother, Trey, and—much to the delight of area coaches—he developed a passion for football. He enrolled in a junior NFL camp, never once complaining about the heat, the rigorous practice schedule, or the endless hits that he took. One day, after a particularly rough play, Duncan tried to get up and discovered that he couldn't walk. "Coach," he said calmly, "I think I hurt my knee."

Duncan, at age fourteen, had broken his left femur. Three screws in his leg and an entire summer filled with rehab left him eager to get back into the game, and when school started again in the fall, the high school coaches were equally ready to see him back on the field. Duncan soon found himself in the starting lineup, calling the plays for the team.

"Can you believe it?" Kenzie said to her husband, Will, as they watched their freshman son from the stands. "He's having the time of his life!"

Suddenly, though, Kenzie's delight at watching her son play turned to concern. A player had gone down. Knowing—knowing!—that Duncan couldn't possibly be on the field at that point, she searched the sidelines for his jersey. She couldn't find him. She turned her attention back to the field just as the downed player's helmet was removed. Kenzie grabbed Will's arm in disbelief. It was Duncan.

This time, he couldn't move. Kenzie and Will raced onto the field, along with a host of coaches and athletic trainers. It was obvious that Duncan had broken his other leg—and that this break was much worse than the first. With his head in Will's lap, Duncan cried out in agony, and then, in the hour that it took for the ambulance to locate the football field, he struggled to maintain consciousness. "Hang on, Dunc," Will urged, silently willing the paramedics to hurry.

When they finally got Duncan to the hospital, doctors put four more pins into his body—this time into his right leg.

"Here we go again," Kenzie thought to herself, dreading the months of rehab that undoubtedly lay ahead. Duncan, she knew, would hate being sidelined during his freshman season.

But sitting on the sidelines turned out to be the least of Duncan's worries. Three days after coming home from the hospital, he began to have trouble breathing. "We need to get you checked out," Kenzie said, struggling to keep the concern out of her voice as they drove the all-too-familiar route to the hospital.

Duncan, the doctors discovered, had a life-threatening pulmonary embolism.

At this point, I need to interrupt the story to tell you that, when it comes to trusting God, Kenzie is probably the most steadfast woman I know. Several years ago, when a medical resident (mistakenly, it turned out) thought that Kenzie had breast cancer and began to cry in the examining room, Kenzie was the one who refused to be shaken. "You need to pull yourself together!" she admonished the distraught young doctor. "It's going to be all right—but you will *never* be able to help your patients if you act like this!"

That steadfastness turned out to be critical, as Kenzie and Will spent the next six days by Duncan's side, watching him wage a life-and-death battle to breathe. Her eyes on the monitors, Kenzie learned to count respirations and heartbeats by the minute. When the time came to remove Duncan's cast in an attempt to find the source of the embolism—a procedure that was guaranteed to be both frightening and painful—she retreated to the hallway to pray, leaving Will to stay by Duncan's side.

Tears streaming down her face, Kenzie fell to the floor to intercede for her son. She cried out to the Lord—and then without warning, she heard his voice in reply: *This will be a pivotal time in Duncan's life.* To Kenzie, "pivotal" meant that Duncan's injury would mark a turning point in his life—and that he would not die.

Duncan spent the next six days in the hospital and was put on a blood thinner to prevent additional clotting. Kenzie suspected that he would return to school in a wheelchair, and when the doctor insisted that he use crutches instead, she blanched. In her mind, the opportunity for additional injury was far greater for a boy on crutches than for one who was safely ensconced in a chair. She understood the doctor's concern—that the use of a wheelchair might lead to a permanent lack of mobility in Duncan's knee—but her mother's intuition told her that crutches were a bad idea.

Sure enough, Duncan had only been back at school for a few days when he slipped on a wet tile floor as he tried to open a door, rebreaking his femur. Doctors set the bone again and sent Duncan home to recover—only this time the pain did not subside. He seemed to be slipping away.

A call to the orthopedic surgeon netted a prescription for painkillers, which Will hurried to the pharmacy to fetch. Sitting by her son's bedside, Kenzie asked if there was anything else she could do. "Mom," Duncan pleaded, "please just pray!"

Kenzie did—and heard God's voice a second time: *Don't mask this pain.* She realized that Duncan was going into shock—he had clammy skin, a rapid pulse, and eyes that could not focus—and that drugs were not what he needed. She called 911.

Back at the hospital, they learned that Duncan was bleeding internally. His leg—and his life—was in serious danger.

Doctors scheduled another operation, which they warned that Duncan might not survive. "Lord," Kenzie prayed, "you said this would be a pivotal time in Duncan's life. All I can do is pray. Save him, God."

The surgery was successful. The bleeding stopped, and from that point on, Duncan began to improve. He moved from his bed and then to his wheelchair—which his buddies had customized with everything from flags and pinwheels to cushions and a cup holder—and then to the physical therapist's office.

A year later, Duncan was wrestling on the varsity squad.

He still bears the scars from his ordeal—both on his legs and in his memory. Likewise, Kenzie still cries sometimes when she talks about her son's brush with death. But what moves her to tears even more is the tender way that God cared for their family, drawing close in their darkest moments to reassure them of his presence. He showed them, as God showed the Israelites in Joshua 1:9, how to be strong and courageous—rather than terrified or discouraged—because he was with them, no matter what.

"I don't know why God allowed Duncan to get hurt," Kenzie says, "but I know that he used the experience to reveal himself to us and to our boys and to teach us about the importance of prayer. Seeing Trey kneel beside Duncan's bed and pray for him, or listening to them talk and laugh when Trey would come home at night and regale Duncan with the goings-on in the teenage world, watching them grow closer to each other and to the Lord—those are the images that I will remember. As difficult as it was, Duncan's injury is not, first and foremost, a painful memory. It is an amazing testimony of God's love."

Prayer Principle

When we realize that God is more concerned
with spiritual victories than athletic victories,
the most painful experiences often become the
most beautiful testimonies of his love.

Poised for Prayer

While writing this chapter, I asked Hillary which sports she thought were the most dangerous. "Well," she said, "you can get tackled in football or hit by a ball in baseball or lacrosse. You can pull something out of a socket while you are wrestling, hit your head while you are diving, or just drown in the pool. Every sport is dangerous. But that's part of the fun."

(Have I mentioned lately how teens and parents tend to see things differently?)

I haven't asked, but I'm guessing that Kenzie didn't see the potential danger in her son's football career as "part of the fun." Listening to her story and thinking of Duncan's courage as he faced one medical hurdle and athletic setback after another, I couldn't help but wonder about all the times when our prayers for our teen's safety and protection seem to go unanswered. God *did* spare Duncan's life, but did he have to put him on the bench—or more specifically, in a wheelchair or on crutches— for nearly two years?

In a similar vein, it hasn't been a whole lot of fun to pray for my own teens—and then watch them perform poorly or get cut from a team or play for a coach whose methods they (and I) might not understand. Intellectually, I realize that these things are often part of the character-building process, but sometimes I find myself asking God what he is really *doing* in the big picture of their lives.

Scripture tells the story of three teens—strapping young men named Shadrach, Meshach, and Abednego—who found their faith tested by circumstances far more intimidating than broken bones and crazy coaches. When these guys refused to play by the king's rules—bowing down to worship his ninety-foot-tall golden statue—he didn't make them run extra laps or sit out for the second half. He ordered that they be thrown into a blazing furnace—immediately.

Had I been in their shoes—or more to the point, had I been one of their mothers—I feel quite certain that I would have staged some sort of protest, or at least hollered for a ref. I would have been shocked, angry, and thoroughly terrified!

But these boys took a different approach. They looked at the king and said, "The God we serve is able to save us from the furnace and from your hand, O king. But even if he does not, we want you to know, O king, that we will not serve your gods or worship the image of gold you have set up."[1]

As parents, we can learn a lot from Shadrach, Meshach, and Abednego. They trusted God completely—without reservation and to the point where their very lives were at stake. If we can do the same thing as we pray for our teenage athletes—asking God to protect them but recognizing that his ultimate goal is to draw them closer to himself and win a spiritual victory in their lives—we can sit on the sidelines, cheering (and praying) for our kids with confidence and peace.

---

1. Daniel 3:17–18.

Prayers You Can Use

Heavenly Father,

As the mountains surround Jerusalem, please surround _____ with your protection, now and forevermore.

PSALM 125:2

Watch over _____. Do not let his foot slip, and keep him from all harm. Thank you for being a God who neither slumbers not sleeps but always watches over my child.

PSALM 121:3–8

Remind _____ of the value of strict training. Help her to run in such a way as to get the prize—both in athletics, where the victor's crown is temporal, and in the bigger game of life, and as she pursues a crown that will last forever.

1 CORINTHIANS 9:24–25

When _____ struggles with athletic disappointment or injury, remind him that you have plans to prosper him and to give him hope for the future. Prompt _____ to pray, especially during seasons of discouragement, and listen to him when he calls to you.   JEREMIAH 29:11–12

When _____ goes through trials in her athletic career, use them to refine her faith. Let her come out of this painful season with a faith that is steadfast and genuine so that she will bring honor and glory to you. 1 PETER 1:6–7

Help _____ to remember that his opponents may be strong in the flesh, but that you, Lord, are with him to help him and to fight his battles. 2 CHRONICLES 32:8

Give _____ strength and increase her power. Cause her to put her hope in you, and renew her strength as she waits on you. Let her soar on wings like eagles and run without growing weary. ISAIAH 40:29–31

As _____ runs the race of life, let him throw off sin and run with perseverance. Let him keep his eyes fixed on Jesus, so that he will not grow weary and lose heart.

HEBREWS 12:1–3

Help _____ not to be afraid. Let her stand firm and trust in you. Whether she is competing on the athletic field or waging a battle against sickness or injury, remind her that you are the God who fights for her. EXODUS 14:13–14

Cover _____ and be his shield. Command your angels to guard him when he is on the field. Rescue him and protect him, and answer him when he calls on you.

PSALM 91:4, 11, 14–15

Let _____ be glad for all that you are planning for her. Help her to be patient when she is not getting as much playing time as she might want, and remind her to always be prayerful.   ROMANS 12:12

When _____ enjoys an athletic victory or accomplishment, prompt him to give you the credit. Let him know that you are the one who gives strength and power, and that everything he has—including his athletic talent and ability—comes from your hand.   1 CHRONICLES 29:12–14

CHAPTER 14

Praying for Healing from Eating Disorders

"I am the LORD, who heals you."
EXODUS 15:26

Our daughter Annesley is a peer counselor at her school. Her job isn't to fix people's problems or give advice; rather, she is mainly supposed to be an available and willing listener. The school has a professional counselor on staff, as well as an extensive network of referral options, but the peer counseling program provides a confidential and nonthreatening entry point for students who need help sorting through their options, with the hope that they'll be better equipped to solve their own problems.

Sometimes, though, professional help is warranted. To help peer counselors know when to make referrals, they participate in a training program designed to familiarize them with all sorts of teenage issues, from sexually transmitted diseases and teenage pregnancy to drug abuse, self-injury, and suicide. When I asked Annesley which aspect of the training had been the most valuable, she didn't hesitate.

"Eating disorders," she said. "They gave us so much good information about the signs and causes and treatment options.

Plus, out of all of the problems we covered, eating disorders are probably the most realistic."

Translation: To Annesley's way of thinking, eating disorders are among the most common problems her peers might face.

That didn't surprise me. Preparing to write this chapter, I learned that incidences of anorexia (self-induced starvation) and bulimia (binging and purging for weight control)—almost unheard-of when I was in high school—are growing at an alarming rate. Although these disorders affect both men and women from all races, ages, and socioeconomic backgrounds, the vast majority—90 percent according to one study—of people who suffer from anorexia or bulimia are women between the ages of twelve and twenty-five.[1]

Given the appearance-obsessed attitude of our culture, the increasing prevalence of eating disorders is understandable. Can you guess what the number one wish is for girls aged eleven to seventeen? It's to be thinner! Teen-oriented magazines that once offered articles like "Snag a Guy! Bake Him a Pie!" are now filled with weight-loss gimmicks and pictures of impossibly thin women in scanty clothing. And researchers have found that women who looked at these magazine photos showed more signs of depression and were more dissatisfied with their bodies after only one to three minutes of viewing the pictures.[2]

No wonder Annesley says that the problem is realistic!

1. National Alliance for the Mentally Ill, 2003 (statistics cited at the National Mental Health Information Center (see mentalhealth.samhsa.gov/publications/allpubs/ken98-0047/default.asp).
2. See Vicki Courtney, *Your Girl: Raising a Godly Daughter in an Ungodly World* (Nashville: Broadman & Holman, 2004), 72.

As I reviewed some research on eating disorders — noting the contributing factors (such things as social pressure to be thin, family stress, emotional insecurities, a tendency toward perfectionism, and so on), as well as the accompanying medical problems (changes in brain size, bone and muscle mass, menstrual cycles, heart and liver functions, and a host of other scary stuff) — I found myself growing more and more discouraged. I thought about our own daughters and their precious friends, many of whom have bought into the lie that their self-worth is tied to the way they look — and that the thinner they are, the better. I wondered how best to pray for these girls, and what I could say to encourage them.

And then I talked to a mother named Debra, whose story gave me a reason to hope ...

"Mom, can I go for a run?"

"Olivia!" Debra replied, "It's ten o'clock! It's pitch-dark outside."

"I know, Mom, but I need a study break. Pleeeeease."

Teenage girls! Debra shook her head, half wondering whether she would make it through Debra's senior year. Even as she grumbled, though, she rummaged around for a sweater in the closet. If Olivia was going to go for a run, she wasn't going to go alone. Debra didn't intend to suit up; rather, she planned to stick her head out the door and keep watch.

"I'll tell you what," she offered. "You can run down to the Johnsons' house and back."

"Mom! That's just four houses away!"

"I know. You can go back and forth a hundred times if you want to. Take it or leave it."

Olivia took it—just as Debra knew she would. That girl could not go a day without some form of serious exercise.

As Olivia beat a path up and down their street, Debra found her thoughts running just as fast. Anyone would say that Olivia had a cute figure—all traces of her pre-adolescent pudginess had vanished—but she was definitely more than a little concerned about her weight. As a middle schooler, she had started packing her own lunches to ensure that they weren't too fattening. By the time she hit high school, what began as a novelty had become an obsession. Debra would never forget the family vacation where Olivia's refusal to eat hot dogs and potato chips had transformed a low-key lunch into a tearful, angry scene.

Counseling helped, but Debra sensed that the therapists they talked with didn't really understand the issues behind eating disorders. They seemed to be more concerned with treating Olivia's physical symptoms than with helping her to overcome any anxiety or emotional hurts she might be carrying. Similarly, the medical community didn't appear to be overly worried about Olivia's health. At five feet seven inches tall and weighing just 106 pounds, Olivia was definitely thin, but a doctor had assured Debra that she was "OK." Debra wanted to believe that he was right.

Now, as Olivia returned from her run, Debra found herself wondering what the future might hold. It would only be a few months before Olivia went off to college. As a mother, Debra had watched her daughter so carefully—keeping tabs on her late-night runs was just one example of her maternal diligence—and she knew she would have to give Olivia some space. Difficult as it may be, she resolved not to become one of those overprotective mothers who called to check up on her child all the time. Rather, she wanted to let her little girl enjoy a taste of independence.

But several months later, when Olivia came home for Thanksgiving, Debra knew that she had a serious problem. Olivia's younger sister, Bess, heard her throwing up in the bathroom, and it quickly became apparent to everyone, including the visiting grandparents, that Olivia had found yet another way—beyond limiting her food intake and exercising compulsively—to keep her weight down.

Always a praying mom, Debra redoubled her efforts. Using verses such as 2 Corinthians 10:4, she prayed against the stronghold of vanity, and of any obsessive-compulsive behaviors that might have taken root in Olivia's life. With verses such as Romans 12:1–2, she asked God to renew Olivia's mind and transform her thoughts so that she would see her body as something that was holy and pleasing to God. And fearful that she might say the wrong thing as she tried to encourage her daughter to make healthy choices, Debra clung to passages such as Isaiah 51:16, trusting in God to put his words in her mouth—even as he kept them safe under the protection of his hand.

Gradually, through Debra's prayers and the help of a cousin who encouraged her to take better care of herself, Olivia began to gain a little bit of weight and didn't balk at what she saw in the mirror. She still struggled with anxiety, though, and—after a bout of depression and a relationship with a fellow she *thought* she was going to marry—she discovered that she was pregnant.

The dating relationship ended. Knowing that she would keep her baby, Olivia took a year off from school.

"Olivia had a great pregnancy," Debra says, somewhat wryly. "She was amazingly fit, working out every day. We even stopped at a twenty-four-hour fitness center en route to the hospital so that she could get in one last workout before the baby came!"

Today, little Sarah is the light of Olivia's life. Olivia no longer starves herself, and by the time this book is published, she will have earned her college degree. Thinking of her little girl—and of the countless impressionable young girls she will be growing up with—Olivia aims to become a registered dietician so she can, as she puts it, "help young girls learn to control their weight in a *healthy* way instead of taking the drastic measures I did."

For her part, Debra is continuing to pray—and to babysit when Olivia wants to hit the gym. "Without the Lord," she says, "I think I would think, like the rest of the world, that Olivia will always have an eating disorder—either limiting her calories or overexercising to keep the weight off. But with God, all things are possible! He is the one who is renewing Olivia's mind, rekindling her faith, and drawing her back. I am counting on him to completely deliver her—and when he is in control, and not the eating disorder, then she will be a prisoner set free!"

Thank God for what he has done in your teen's life —
and believe for the answers
to prayer that are yet to come.

Poised for Prayer

I have to tell you that, as I talked with Debra, I couldn't help myself. Listening to her so candidly recount the details of their story, I was amazed by the peace and joy that flowed through the telephone wires. I *had* to ask the question. "Debra," I said, "You sound like an amazing mother. You seem so, so — *fine* about everything. If I had a daughter who asked me to stop at the gym when she was in labor, I think I might go a little bonkers. How can you be so *patient?*"

"Oh, goodness — I am definitely not patient!" Debra laughed. "I have been mad and scared and frustrated. I've cried buckets of tears, and Olivia and I have certainly had plenty of arguments — especially when I think she's making a bad choice or taking an unnecessary risk. I *still* struggle with whether to make a cake or not, or whether to tell Olivia that she looks great when she says she's lost two pounds. I worry that I'll be too controlling or that I'll say the wrong thing.

"But I *do* trust God. I've asked him to put his words in my mouth, and I rely on his strength and wisdom every day as I pray for my daughter. One of my favorite things to do is to read my Bible and find Scriptures I can pray that match our specific needs — God's Word is just *so* important."

Obviously, I couldn't agree more. And if your daughter is struggling with an eating disorder—or, for that matter, any sort of dissatisfaction with her appearance, from disliking her nose to wishing that she had naturally straight (or curly) hair—take a moment to read through Psalm 139. Tell her that she is "fearfully and wonderfully made" and that God created her to be just the way she is. Look up Psalm 45:11, and remind your girl that the king—her King—is *enthralled* by her beauty! And above all, help her to see that when her identity is rooted in how God sees her—and not in what our crazy culture says—then she won't have to worry about growing up and getting wrinkles or stretch marks or putting on a couple of pounds. "Beauty," as Proverbs 31:30 so deftly puts it, "is fleeting; but a woman who fears the LORD"—and who anchors her self-worth firmly in his love—"is to be praised."

Finally, don't be afraid to seek professional advice. Even as I cringed over the symptoms and medical complications—some of them life-threatening—that can accompany anorexia and bulimia, I was greatly encouraged to read about the treatment options for eating disorders, as well as by the recovery rate for those who get help.[1]

Like Debra, you may not always know what to do or what to say. But God does. As you pray for your daughter, depend on his faithfulness, his love, and his word. As Debra would happily tell you, there's no better place to put your trust.

---

1. For more information about eating disorders, please see the appendix and the appropriate recommended resources.

Prayers You Can Use

Heavenly Father,

Let _____ know that you have made her and formed her, and that all your ways are perfect. Nourish her the way you nourished the Israelites, and keep her safe in your hand.

DEUTERONOMY 32:4, 6b, 12, 39

When _____ feels anxious, be her security and her shield, and let her rest between your shoulders. Lead her into a land of safety, a land where she can see the grain and new wine — the food and drink you provide — as a gift rather than something to be feared or abused.

DEUTERONOMY 33:12, 28

Remind _____ that you do not look at the things that human beings look at — such as outward appearance — but that you value what's in her heart.   1 SAMUEL 16:7

Keep your eyes on _____. Cause her to hope in your unfailing love, and deliver her from death. Keep her alive, even during times of self-imposed famine.   PSALM 33:18–19

Bring your peace to _____'s heart because a heart at peace gives life to the body.   PROVERBS 14:30

Let _____ feast on your Word. Let the words of Scripture be her joy and her delight, and let her bear the name of you, the Lord God Almighty. JEREMIAH 15:16

You are the God of peace. Please make _____ holy in every way, letting her whole spirit, soul, and body be kept blameless until Jesus comes again. Lord, you are faithful; you will do this. 1 THESSALONIANS 5:23–24

Direct _____'s thoughts so that she will set her mind on things above, not on earthly things, such as her weight or how she looks. Help her put to death those things that belong to her earthly nature, including her obsession with her body, which is a form of idolatry. COLOSSIANS 3:2, 5

As I speak to _____ about her weight or anything else, please help my words to be kind. Let them be like honey—sweet to the soul and healthy for the body.

PROVERBS 16:24

Set _____ free from the prison of her distorted self-image, that she may praise your name. PSALM 142:7

Bless _____ and keep her; make your face shine upon her. Be gracious to her, and give her peace.

NUMBERS 6:24–26

Search _____, and know her thoughts. Protect her, and place your hand of blessing on her life. Let her know that she is fearfully and wonderfully made, and that when you look at her—as you have done since even before she was born—you see your beautiful workmanship.

PSALM 139:1, 5, 13–14

When _____ suffers affliction and loathes all food, prompt her to cry out to you and save her from her distress.

PSALM 107:17–19

I pray that out of your glorious riches you will strengthen _____ with power through your Spirit in her inner being.

EPHESIANS 3:16

CHAPTER 15

Praying for Healing from Self-Injury

You are the children of the LORD your God.
Do not cut yourselves . . . .
The LORD has chosen you to be his treasured possession.
DEUTERONOMY 14:1–2

I first heard about the practice of "cutting" about five years ago, when we lived in southern California. A couple of middle school girls had been seen with razor marks on their arms, and although I knew the girls only by name, my heart ached for them and for their families. I couldn't imagine what they must have been feeling—to want to hurt themselves that way.

Back then, I thought that the girls' behavior was an isolated incident, one of those "out there" things that a kid growing up in the shadow of Hollywood might decide to try. Not long ago, though, I heard a radio host say that a recent poll showed that about 20 percent of the students at Ivy League universities had cut or otherwise injured themselves. These students saw it, the radio host explained, as a way to cope with stress in their lives.

If I still had any doubt that self-injury had become a mainstream issue in our culture, it vanished as I began working on this chapter. I was talking with a sixth grader—one of the girls from our youth group at church—and out of the blue, she told me that one of her classmates had used a needle to slash her arms. A sixth grader!

I decided to do a little digging. I called the folks at Teen Mania Ministries, a group that has spent the past twenty years working with teens at stadium events, missionary expeditions, and other outreach and discipleship oriented activities. From the research they shared, I learned that cutting—along with biting, pinching, burning, and other forms of self-mutilation—has been tried by as many as 40 percent of today's teens, particularly young women, who tend to internalize hurt and pain rather than resort to outward displays of aggression the way young men more often do.[1]

Those findings would come as no surprise to my friend Karen. When she learned that I was writing this book, she told me her story ...

Natalie hung up the phone, anger and hurt boiling inside of her. She had tried to help her friend, to make her see that having sex with her boyfriend was not a good idea, but it was no use. Rachel didn't want to hear it, and their heated conversation had made one thing perfectly clear: not only was she rejecting Natalie's advice; she was rejecting her friendship.

Grabbing her tennis racquet, Natalie headed outside, slamming the door behind her. *Whack! Whack! Whack!* She smacked the ball against the garage door, over and over again,

---

1. For more information on the help that Teen Mania offers, please see the appendix in the back of this book.

tears blurring her vision. She was just so *angry!* Stooping to pick up the ball, she felt as though she would explode. She slammed her fist into the stucco wall.

Her knuckles were ripped and bloody, but Natalie didn't care. Right now, she hated Rachel. She hated herself. Why had she even said anything? So much for the Bible's command to "speak the truth in love."[1] When it came to friendships, speaking the truth could be far too costly.

Natalie went back inside, now more hurt than angry. She knew a couple of girls at school who had cut themselves, saying that it gave them a sense of control over their emotions. At first, Natalie had thought they were weird; now she wasn't so sure. Maybe they knew something she didn't.

Natalie opened the cabinet above her sink, searching for something sharp. Would a disposable razor work? She didn't know — and frankly, she didn't care. Right now, she just wanted to find an outlet for her pain. She drew the blade across the back of her hand and watched, transfixed, as the blood came. It hurt, but in a strange way it also felt like a release. She pressed the razor into her other hand.

The next morning, a series of angry red lines were all that remained of Natalie's rage. She managed to leave the house without anyone seeing the marks, but they weren't so easy to hide at school. A friend alerted the school counselor, who called Natalie into his office.

That night, Natalie told her parents, Karen and Tom, what she had done.

Karen was as stunned as she was confused. Natalie was a gifted athlete, the president of her sophomore class, and a

---

1. Ephesians 4:15.

vibrant Christian who served as a leader in her church's youth group. Not only that, but she was gorgeous. To look at her, no one would ever guess that anything could be wrong in her life!

Karen felt as though she had failed as a mother. "When I saw Natalie's hands," she told me, "all I could think about was that these were the same hands I kissed that day in the hospital when she was born. They were the hands that had slipped into mine when she was a little girl, as the two of us looked for shells on the beach. They were beautiful hands—and they still are—only now they look angry and scarred. What was going on inside my baby girl? Why would she want to hurt herself?"

I didn't have any answers, but I promised to join Karen and Tom as they asked God for wisdom and insight. A few days later, Karen called me again. This time, her voice was filled with excitement.

"We took Natalie to see a professional counselor," she said, "and the woman helped us understand some of the things that might be going on in Natalie's mind. But you know me. I want to be sure that God is in this too. I need to know that he's got everything under control. I need a *Scripture!*"

"Yes," I replied, knowing exactly how Karen felt.

"Well, listen to this!" she continued. "I was reading my Bible this morning, and I came across Isaiah 49:15. Here's what it says: 'Can a mother forget the baby at her breast and have no compassion on the child she has borne? Though she may forget, I will not forget you!' When I read those words, I knew that God was speaking to me, saying that he loves Natalie and that he will never forget her. He has everything under control."

"He does!" I agreed.

"But that's not even the best part. Listen to verse 16: It says, 'I have engraved you on the palms of my hands.'"

I have engraved you on the palms of my hands.

I heard Karen's voice, and I could read her mind: the Almighty God of the universe had Natalie's name carved into the palms of his hands, written in the precious blood of his only Son.

"I know that Natalie's hands were marked by anger," Karen said softly as we finished our conversation. "But God's hands are marked by love."

Prayer Principle

God will never forget your child.
Her name is engraved on the palms of his hands.

Karen and Tom continued to pray, asking God in his infinite wisdom to find a way to bring good out of Natalie's pain. One night, several weeks later, Karen slipped into Natalie's room to kiss her good-night. She found her daughter propped up in bed, an open Bible on her lap.

"Hey Mom," Natalie said, "Do you know what it says in James 1:2?"

"Tell me," Karen prompted.

"It says we're supposed to consider it 'pure joy' whenever we face trials, because God uses them to test our faith and make us complete. I've had a lot of trials this year—"

"Mm-hmm," Karen agreed, waiting for her daughter to continue.

"So I guess it's all good. I mean, God is going to use the bad stuff to bring about good stuff. And that gives me joy."

Karen wanted to say something, but her emotion choked her words. Through one simple verse, God had filled her daughter's heart with joy. With a few simple words, she had found a new reason to hope. And in one simple moment, Karen knew that God had answered her prayers — showing her yet again, through the words of Scripture, that he really was in control.

Poised for Prayer

When Karen told me her story, she said that one of the hardest things for her was that she couldn't understand what was going on inside Natalie's mind and that she felt so ill-equipped to help her daughter. This has been a common refrain as I've talked with parents in recent months. When teens struggle — whether the problem involves self-injury, peer relationships, suicide attempts, or something else — there are plenty of times when parents don't understand what is happening, and we don't always know how we can help. Many times, too, we aren't even sure how best to pray.

The good news is that God knew there'd be days — and even entire seasons — like that. During those uncertain times, we can turn to the Holy Spirit, our helper. I love how Romans 8:26 reads in the NLT: "The Holy Spirit helps us in our distress. For we don't even know what we should pray for, nor how we should pray. But the Holy Spirit prays for us with groanings that cannot be expressed in words."

Isn't it good to know that the God who searches our hearts — and those of our teens — knows exactly what is needed? As parents, we can turn to him in our times of greatest weakness and confusion, knowing that not only will his Spirit *help* us, but that he will even go so far as to *pray* for us!

And two verses later, in Romans 8:28 (NLT), the promise gets even better. God says that he will cause everything—even the bewildering, frustrating, and difficult stuff—to work together for the good of those who love him and are called according to his purpose.

Like you, I want God's best for my kids. And as I reflect on these verses, I cannot imagine a greater privilege than that of joining our human hearts and longings together with the mind of the Holy Spirit, trusting in the power of prayer as we ask God to place his protective arms around our teens and accomplish his beautiful purposes in their lives.

Prayers You Can Use

Heavenly Father,

You are the God of peace. Make _____ holy in every way, keeping her whole spirit, soul, and body blameless until that day when our Lord Jesus Christ comes again.

1 THESSALONIANS 5:23

Let _____ take refuge in you and be glad; let him ever sing for joy. Spread your protection over _____ that he may rejoice in you. PSALM 5:11

Let _____ know that she belongs to you and that her heart can be at rest in your presence. When her heart tries to condemn her, remind her of this truth: you are greater than our hearts, and you know everything. 1 JOHN 3:19–20

Keep _____ from all harm. Watch over her life; watch over her coming and going, both now and forevermore.

PSALM 121:7–8

I pray that _____'s identity will be firmly rooted and established in Christ's love, and that he will grasp how wide and long and high and deep is the love that you have for him. EPHESIANS 3:17–18

*Record _____'s lament and list her tears on your scroll.
Let her know that you are for her and that she does not need
to be afraid.*   PSALM 56:9–11

*Let _____ see that he has been chosen by you and that
he belongs to you. Equip him to declare your praises because
you have called him out of darkness into your wonderful
light.*   1 PETER 2:9

*Do not let _____ be anxious about anything, but as
she presents her concerns to you, fill her with your peace.
Guard her heart and her mind.*   PHILIPPIANS 4:6–7

*Help _____ to realize that his body is a temple where
the Holy Spirit lives, and that it belongs to you, Lord God.
Remind _____ that he was bought at a price and that
he should honor you in the way he treats his body.*

                                            1 CORINTHIANS 6:19–20

*Gently remind _____ that even if it seems as though
everyone has forgotten or neglected her, you never will. Let
her know that her name is engraved on the palms of your
hands.*   ISAIAH 49:15–16

Let _____ find joy in even the most painful circumstances, knowing that you use the troubles in his life to develop endurance and strengthen his character so that he will be ready for anything.   JAMES 1:2−4

Keep _____ from cutting herself or hurting herself in anyway. Let her know, beyond the shadow of a doubt, that you have chosen her—and that she is your treasured possession.   DEUTERONOMY 14:1−2

Replace _____'s tears with joy, and fan the gifts you have given him into flame. Remind him that you have not given him a spirit of timidity, but of power, love, and self-discipline.   2 TIMOTHY 1:4−7

May the grace of the Lord Jesus Christ be with _____'s spirit.   PHILIPPIANS 4:23

CHAPTER 16

Praying Your Teen through Depression

This is what God promises:

to bestow on [us] a crown of beauty
*   instead of ashes,*
the oil of gladness
*   instead of mourning,*
and a garment of praise
*   instead of a spirit of despair.*

ISAIAH 61:3

When my father had the blues, he used to say that he felt "lower than whale vomit." Whale vomit, he told me, sinks to the bottom of the ocean; in other words, it's down about as far as you can get.

I'm no marine biologist, and I can't vouch for the accuracy of my dad's claims, but I'm guessing that Jonah knew a little something about the subject. Shortly after the big fish barfed him onto the beach, Jonah found himself in a full-scale pout — but it wasn't because of the whale. Jonah was miffed that God hadn't wiped out the city of Ninevah like Jonah had warned. "Just kill me now, LORD!" he said. "I'd rather be dead than alive because nothing I predicted is going to happen."[1]

---

1. Jonah 4:3 NLT.

Jonah is just one of the Bible's many moaners and groaners. Check out David's complaint: "My bones are weak, my body is tired, and even my soul is exhausted. My neighbors don't like me, and my friends have forgotten me — it's like they think I'm as useless as a broken dish." Or how about Naomi, Ruth's mother-in-law: "Don't call me 'Pleasant'; call me 'Bitter,' because that's my life." Or the prophet Elijah, the fellow who called down fire from heaven, did away with nine hundred false prophets, outran a chariot with his cloak tucked into his belt, and then, exhausted and alone, plopped down under a tree and went to sleep. "I've had enough," he said — and he prayed that God would end his life.[1]

I don't know about you, but I take a sort of perverse "misery loves company" pleasure in knowing that God's people — his *Bible* people — knew what it was like to wrestle with fear, loneliness, exhaustion, disappointment, bitterness, grief, and depression. Even so, it can be tough when these difficult emotions weasel their way into our lives — and even harder when they leap onto the backs of our teens.

My friend Camille is a joyful, energetic mom-on-the-go. Two of her three teens generally share her upbeat outlook, but the third — Hailey — is much quieter. For a while, Camille put Hailey's behavior down to a naturally reserved nature coupled with occasional bouts of teenage moodiness. But as the pieces of the puzzle started coming together, Camille realized that there might be something much deeper — and more frightening — going on ...

---

1. See Psalm 31:9 – 12; Ruth 1:20; 1 Kings 19:3 – 5.

Camille picked up the potato chip bag and dropped the soda can she had found next to the television set into the recycle bin. She wanted to chastise Hailey—both for leaving her trash around and for the poor dietary choices she seemed to be making—but she bit her tongue. Teens were supposed to be slobs and eat junk food, right? It wasn't Hailey's fault that she happened to be born into a household that included a neatnik mother.

When she noticed the lump on the couch, however, Camille decided to speak up. "Hey, Hails," she said, patting the blanket where she figured her daughter's rump would be. "Why don't you get up and go for a run? Or go out and shoot some baskets. It's a beautiful day—and you know what Coach Higgins said. You all are supposed to be working out on the weekends."

"Maybe later," Hailey mumbled, pulling the blanket tighter over her head. "I'm too tired right now."

Camille was glad that Hailey couldn't see her face. She was worried—very much so. A year or so ago, Hailey's academic performance had started to slip. Normally an honor student, she had brought home a disappointing report card, and one of the teachers had observed that Hailey had seemed to have "lost interest" in her schoolwork. Not only that, but Hailey seemed to have also lost interest in her friends. When they called or dropped by, Hailey often responded with indifference or apathy—traits, her mother acknowledged, that wouldn't make other kids want to be around her.

Camille and her husband, Sam, considered their options. They could put Hailey in a private school, where she might find herself more academically and socially engaged. They could talk to a professional counselor. And they could pray.

Camille opted to start with prayer. "Lord," she said, "my heart is breaking for my precious daughter. She seems so sad and lonely; I just don't know what to do."

Two days later, Camille sensed God speaking to her as she read her Bible. The words of Deuteronomy 20:3–4, originally given to the Israelites as they prepared for battle, seemed to jump off the page: "Do not be fainthearted or afraid; do not be terrified or give way to panic before them. For the LORD your God is the one who goes with you to fight for you against your enemies to give you victory."

I know the problem looks huge, God whispered to Camille's heart, *but don't be afraid. Don't panic. Just get out of the way, and let me fight the battle.*

Encouraged by those words, Camille resolved to quit nagging—and to keep praying. At the same time, she and Sam had read about the signs of depression—such things as an inability to concentrate, declining academic performance, a loss of friends, increased fatigue, and mood swings—and they decided it would be prudent to meet with a professional counselor.

"Hailey is definitely minimizing things in her life," the woman said when they met privately after she had talked with Hailey. "Is there any family history of depression?"

Camille felt her heart skip a beat. Both her mother and Sam's mother had been treated for depression, but they had discounted any possible connection to Hailey's situation, figuring that an older woman's problems were nothing like what a teen might be going through.

"I'm not overly concerned," the counselor reassured them, "but I definitely see signs of mild depression. Let's see how things go—and please don't hesitate to call if you need me."

The ensuing months were difficult ones. Hailey seemed to take two steps forward and one step back, and each time Camille and Sam thought she had turned a corner, something would happen—a fight with a friend, a descent into sullenness, an outburst of aggression—that would drive them to their knees in prayer. Camille desperately wanted to do something to "fix" Hailey's problems, and she hated feeling so helpless. Rather than dwelling on her limitations, though, she decided to focus on God's power and his love. She knew the words of 1 Peter 5:7 by heart—that God invited her to cast all her anxieties on him because he cared for her—and she figured she might as well take him up on his offer.

Camille found herself looking forward to her weekly Moms in Prayer meeting. She loved praying with the other moms and relished the Scripture verses they shared. So often, a particular verse seemed to be written especially for her. On one of Camille's darkest days—she was running late because she had been crying over one of Hailey's outbursts—she slipped into the meeting and arrived just in time to hear one of the women quote Isaiah 46:4: "I have made you and I will carry you; I will sustain you and I will rescue you."

That's what Hailey needs, Camille thought to herself—someone to rescue her; and that's what I need too—someone to carry me.

Time passed, and Hailey seemed—slowly but surely—to be gaining confidence. She made some new friends at church, and as she prepared to go on a retreat with this group, Camille came across a verse that reflected the cry of her heart: "Give us gladness in proportion to our former misery! Replace the evil years with good. Let us see your miracles again; let our children see your glory at work."[1]

"Things have definitely improved," Camille told me not long ago. "Hailey's grades are up, she is enjoying her sports again, and she seems to have made some new friends. But I'm still praying that verse about proportionate gladness. If God is going to give us gladness in proportion to our former misery, then we definitely have some good years ahead!

"I hate to admit it," she continued, "but I think that God has used Hailey's struggles to teach me that I cannot fix everything and that I need to depend on him to work out his will in her life. It's a tough place to be, but I'm learning — slowly — that it's exactly where God wants me."

Prayer Principle

When you find yourself in a place
where all you can do is depend on God, do that —
and count on him to rescue you.

Poised for Prayer

My father — the one with the whale-vomit wisdom — went to be with the Lord in 2001, after a yearlong bout with cancer. Five years later, my mother married a widower named John, a godly man I have come to deeply love and respect. When I told him that I was working on this book, he shared a story that brought tears to my eyes.

---

1. Psalm 90:15 – 16 NLT.

"When I was about twelve years old," John said, "my mother came down with a crippling form of arthritis. Within a year, she was confined to her bed, and I grew up having to change her sheets and do almost everything for her. She never went to any of my school plays or sports events, never helped me with my homework, and couldn't even make a peanut butter and jelly sandwich to put in my lunch.

"The only thing my mother could do was pray. She prayed for me every day—and I knew it. And when I got older and had the opportunity to make some very ungodly decisions, I found that I couldn't do it. I couldn't get away from my mother's prayers and from the memory of what she had done for me day after day, year after year—talking to God as she lay in her bed."

Whether you find yourself impaired by illness or—like my friend Camille—by circumstances that have left you unable to "fix" your teen's problems, don't despair. When you are in a position where all you can do is pray, you are in a powerful place indeed.

Earlier in this chapter, I mentioned David, Naomi, and Elijah. These folks struggled with discouragement and depression—but that's only part of their story. In each instance, God wasn't finished with them yet. They cried out to him in the depths of despair, and he put them back on their feet.

In Elijah's case, God ministered to him with rest—and with some much-needed food and drink—before giving him a new mission.

For Naomi, bitterness gave way to joy as she waited on God to alter her lot in life, which he did—providing Ruth to walk alongside her and Boaz to provide for her — in a beautiful story of faithfulness and redemption.

And for David, the change took place as David adjusted his perspective, focusing less on his problems and more on God's unfailing love and protection. Out of the depths of his discouragement, he summoned his resolve and began to praise God. If you read his song recorded in Psalm 31, you'll see a man who went from anguish and sorrow to one who could say, with confidence and joy, "How great is your goodness, which you have stored up for those who fear you .... Be strong and take heart, all you who hope in the LORD."[1]

Like Elijah, your teen may simply need rest and nourishment. Like Naomi, you may find yourself having to depend on other people — friends and counselors — to be God's arms as he works behind the scenes. Or like David, you (and, for that matter, your teen) may need to shift your focus from problems to praise.

Whatever your circumstance, know that the Lord hears your prayers. Be strong and take heart, and put your hope in the Lord.

He will make a way.

---

1. Psalm 31:19, 24.

Prayers You Can Use

Heavenly Father,

Give _____ beauty for ashes, joy instead of mourning, and praise instead of despair. Comfort her with the promise of your favor, and let her be planted like a strong and graceful oak tree for your own glory.   Isaiah 61:2–3

Hear _____'s cry, Lord. Lift him out of the slimy pit he is in, out of the mud and mire that weighs his heart down. Give him a firm place to stand and put a new song in his mouth—a hymn of praise to you.   Psalm 40:1–3

Search _____, and know her thoughts. Remind her that no matter where she goes or how low she sinks, she cannot hide from your presence. You have not abandoned her; rather you have promised to be with her and to guide her and hold her fast. Let your light shine into the darkness of her life, and show her that, no matter what she thinks or how she perceives herself, you know that she is wonderful.

Psalm 139:1–2, 8–14

Remind _____ that Jesus was despised and rejected by others, and that he was a man of suffering, and familiar with pain. Cause him to cry out for Jesus, knowing that he can cast all of his cares and anxieties on you because you care for him.   ISAIAH 53:3; 1 PETER 5:7

When _____ is in the depths of despair, let her cry out to you. Let your ears be attentive to her cry for mercy. Cause her to put her hope in your word and in your unfailing love, which carries the promise of full redemption — even from these darkest hours.   PSALM 130:1–7

As _____ struggles under the weight of weariness or burdens, remind him that he can come to you and that you will give him rest.   MATTHEW 11:28–30

When _____ finds herself in tears day and night, and when she is sad and discouraged, cause her to put her hope in you and to remember your kindness. Pour out on her your unfailing love throughout each day, and at night fill her heart with your life-giving songs.   PSALM 42:3–8

Thank you for your great love, which will keep _____ from being consumed by discouragement, bitterness, or hopelessness. Thank you for your mercy and your compassion, which is fresh and new every morning. When _____ feels as though all peace and joy are lost, remind him that you are worth waiting for and that you are good to those who put their hope in you.   LAMENTATIONS 3:19–26

Satisfy _____ in the morning with your unfailing love, so that she may sing for joy to the end of her life. Give her gladness in proportion to her former misery! Replace the evil years with good, and let her see your glory at work in her life.   PSALM 90:14–16

Do not let _____ be enslaved by depression or negative emotions. Christ has set him free, so let him stand firm, refusing to let himself be burdened again by a yoke of slavery.   GALATIANS 5:1

Let the light of your face shine on _____. Fill her heart with joy, and let her lie down and sleep in peace.   PSALM 4:6–8

Cause _____ to obey your commands so that he can remain in your love, knowing that as he does, he will be filled with your joy. Let his joy be complete; let him delight in the security of your friendship; and let him remember that you have chosen him to go and bear fruit—fruit that will last.   JOHN 15:10–16

CHAPTER 17

Praying for
Your Teenage Rebel

"My wayward children," says the LORD,
"come back to me,
and I will heal your wayward hearts."
JEREMIAH 3:22 NLT

My friend Rob is a Young Life leader. In addition to interacting with high schoolers on a daily basis, he spends part of almost every summer working at one of the organization's many resort-style camping properties. Young Life's motto is "Every Kid, Everywhere, for Eternity." They take the "Every Kid" part of this charge seriously, dedicating entire outreach programs to virtually every type of teen — from urban tough guys to suburban preppies to unmarried teenage moms.

One of the Young Life ministries, called Capernaum, targets teens with physical and mental disabilities. One summer, Rob found himself working as the speaker at a camp full of Capernaum kids. He told me about one fellow — I'll call him Mac — who absolutely, positively did *not* want to participate in the obstacle course race that had been slated as the evening's activity. Rob walked up just as Mac — who had been swinging his fists at the camp staff and obstinately refusing to accept their assistance—let loose a string of expletives. He was a big guy, and Rob could see the confusion in the staffers' faces as they tried to decide how to respond to the combative teen.

"What should we do?" one of them asked Rob.

"You should help him," Rob said.

"I don't want any help, you blankety-blank blanker!" Mac hollered. "Get away from me!"

"Oh, come on, yes you do—the fun's getting ready to start," Rob smiled, as a couple of the burlier counselors surrounded Mac and began to help him walk.

Eyeing the course—straight up the side of a mountain, in the dark, with logs and rocks and other projectiles designed to impede a climber's progress—Rob hoped that he'd made the right decision. What if Mac really flipped out and tried to take some other kid down with him?

The event began, and—as promised—Mac initially refused to be led up the hill. Once he realized that his companions were not about to give up, though, he resigned himself to the climb. Within moments, it became obvious that he had found a rhythm. As his sullenness gave way to excitement, Mac began pressing forward, leaning on his helpers and urging them on. "Are we gonna win?" he asked again and again. "Are we gonna win?"

As the team reached the top, all traces of obstinacy had disappeared. Mac was joyfully high-fiving his teammates, exulting in the success of their efforts. It wasn't about the win—everyone who finished the climb was a winner as far as the camp was concerned. It was about another kind of victory, the kind that happened because a couple of camp staffers refused to give up on—or stop loving—a kid with a stony heart.

When the time came for Mac to go home, he didn't want to leave. Like the countless teens who had been there before him, he said it was "the best week of his life."

When Rob told me this story, I couldn't help but think of how many "get away from me" teens populate our schools, our neighborhoods, and even our churches. They may not fit the description of a Capernaum kid—someone with a physical or mental disability—but they are every bit as much in need of some "don't give up on me" love.

Lara's daughter, Samantha, was one of those kids. As a seventh grader, Sam began donning black clothing and hanging out with a boy who wore chains, combat boots, and other accessories that marked him as one of the junior high "rebels." Lara and her husband, Peter, didn't care for the boy—or the look—but they hoped that both were part of a passing phase in Samantha's life. But two years later, when Sam ran away from home in the middle of the night, they knew they had a serious problem on their hands ...

Lara's world was spinning out of control. Samantha was gone—and the nightmare was starting again.

Her mind flashed back to the first time Sam had run away, during the summer before her freshman year. A tip from one of Sam's friends led Lara and Peter to call the police, who found Samantha in a house where other young runaways were known to have stopped for shelter. The satanic symbols that marked the walls served as a chilling portent of the home's darker purpose: it served as a gateway to the streets of Los Angeles—and to prostitution.

At the time, Lara had been frantic—and then grateful beyond words that her daughter had been found so quickly. That very day, she and Peter had taken Sam to a counselor, who recommended that she be hospitalized for treatment of depression and low self-esteem. Lara and Peter were stunned: Samantha was a popular, straight-A student. She was athletic, musically talented, and very pretty. Listening to the counselor's diagnosis, Lara had felt her heart sink. She didn't even know how much she didn't know about what was going on inside her precious daughter.

After a month at the treatment center, Sam had come home. The family celebrated her return, and Lara—a lifelong church-goer who had been active in Bible studies for years—had been thrilled by the news that Samantha had recommitted her life to Christ. At last, Lara's dream of having a healthy Christian family seemed within reach.

She and Peter had been fairly strict in the past, fearing that—if things were left up to her—Samantha would make hurtful and potentially life-scarring choices. Maybe, they had thought, it was time to give her some more freedom. But that was easier said than done, particularly when the "friends" that tended to gravitate into Samantha's orbit seemed to be such a troubled, rebellious lot. Trying to talk things out with Samantha rarely helped; more often than not, their conversations had turned into arguments.

Now, looking at the empty bed in Samantha's room, Lara couldn't help but wonder whether they had given her too much freedom. It was the spring of Samantha's junior year—more than two years since the police had brought her home the first time—and she was gone again.

Lara felt like a total failure. Her only consolation was that, unlike the first time she had left, Samantha did not appear to be in imminent danger this time. Taking shelter with whatever school chum would have her (and sometimes sneaking into her boyfriend's house after dark), Samantha showed up for school, continued to get excellent grades, never missed a day of work at her after-school job, and even went to her piano lessons. The only thing she refused to do was to come home.

Knowing that her daughter was nearby did little to ease Lara's pain. What should she and Peter do? Samantha was like a toddler, Lara thought, throwing a temper tantrum whenever the rules got in the way of her desire for independence. If they forced Samantha to come home, she would only run away again.

Lara decided to confide in a few close friends. After hearing what she was going through, one of them mentioned that she had heard about Moms in Prayer on the radio. Praying for their children couldn't hurt; in fact, Lara thought it would be a definite step in the right direction, particularly if she had other mothers who were willing to come alongside to give her strength. Even with Peter sharing the load, her burden had gotten too heavy to bear.

The women began meeting weekly to pray. It didn't take long before Lara realized that something was different. A life-long Christian, she had always believed in prayer, but when this group of moms prayed, they often used Scripture—the actual words in the Bible as the basis for their prayers—and for the first time, Lara began to sense that God's word was alive. She couldn't seem to get enough of it. Even when she wasn't praying with the group, she found herself turning to her Bible, letting the words slip off the pages and into her heart to fill her with strength (Lara's prayers are in italics after the Bible quotations):

> In my distress I called to the LORD;
> I cried to my God for help.
> From his temple he heard my voice;
> my cry came before him....
> He reached down from on high and took hold of me;
> he drew me out of deep waters.
> He rescued me from my powerful enemy,
> from my foes, who were too strong for me.
> They confronted me in the day of my disaster,
> but the LORD was my support.
>
> PSALM 18:6, 16–18

> *"Lord, help us. Rescue me.*
> *Rescue Samantha. Be our support."*

Gently instruct those who oppose the truth. Perhaps God will change those people's hearts, and they will learn the truth. Then they will come to their senses and escape from the devil's trap. For they have been held captive by him to do whatever he wants.

> 2 TIMOTHY 2:25–26 NLT

> *"Teach me, Father, how to reach out*
> *to Samantha. Give her a knowledge of your truth,*
> *and let her escape Satan's trap."*

> When I am afraid,
> I will trust in you.
>
> PSALM 56:3

> *"I do trust you, Lord. I do."*

And then, too, there were passages that seemed to be written expressly for Samantha. Lara hung on these words — praying the Scriptures when it was too painful to pray about the details of her daughter's life — and clung to the hope they provided:

I will ... recapture the hearts of the people of Israel, who have all deserted me for their idols.

EZEKIEL 14:5

> *"Recapture Samantha's heart, Almighty God,*
> *and let her return to you!"*

For the grace of God that brings salvation ... teaches us to say "No" to ungodliness and worldly passions, and to live self-controlled, upright and godly lives in this present age.

TITUS 2:11–12

> *"Shed your grace on her, Lord.*
> *Teach her to say 'No' to her worldly passions*
> *and desires and 'Yes' to the life you desire."*

If you, O LORD, kept a record of sins,
  O Lord, who could stand?
But with you there is forgiveness;
  therefore you are feared.
I wait for the LORD, my soul waits,
  and in his word I put my hope....
Put your hope in the LORD,
  for with the LORD is unfailing love,
  and with him is full redemption.

PSALM 130:3–7

"Thank you, Lord, that you do not keep a record
of Samantha's sin—or of mine. My hope is in your word.
Let Samantha's life—all of our lives—
be fully redeemed by your unfailing love."

Five weeks after she had left, Samantha came home. This time, there was no big celebration—and no dramatic, overnight change. With help from their pastor, Peter and Lara made a covenant with their daughter, a contract that outlined rules and freedoms that came with family life. Samantha agreed to continue in counseling, and Lara continued to pray. God, she knew, had protected Samantha when she and Peter could not; truly, as the psalmist said, God had "reached down from on high" and rescued their family.[1]

Today—more than sixteen years later—Samantha is still a risk taker. She often finds herself in prison and in other dangerous places, only she isn't running anymore. Instead, equipped with a PhD in clinical psychology, she is ministering to those who have found themselves scarred by wrong choices, people whom others have given up trying to help. She loves her family and treats them with appreciation and respect.

"It is so faith-building," Lara says, "to realize that God *was* at work, even when we couldn't see him. He is a faithful, powerful, redeeming God—and without him, we never would have made it through those dark years."

Poised for Prayer

All of the prayer concerns in this book are spiritual battlegrounds, but rebellion is an issue where Satan's hand is often

---

1. Psalm 18:16.

the easiest to see. As the one who comes to "steal and kill and destroy,"[1] he likes nothing more than to rip our families apart, making parents and teens think that their fight is with each other rather than with him.

Lara would be the first to tell you that it isn't easy, but that perseverance — in pursuing your teen, in praying for him or her, and in demonstrating a "don't give up on me" love — is the key to winning this battle. Here's what I mean:

Pursue. Your teen may say that he doesn't want to talk to you and that he doesn't want to do anything with you, but don't close the door on those things. Instead, do everything *you* can do to show that you are interested in his life. Attend sports events and recitals; take him out to breakfast or lunch; ask about his friends, his schoolwork, his activities. If he rebuffs you, don't be discouraged. Take your cues from Hebrews 10:

- stand your ground in the face of suffering, even when you are publicly exposed to insult and persecution (verses 32–33);
- do not throw away your confidence (verse 35);
- and persevere, knowing that when you have done the will of God, you will receive what he has promised (verse 36).

Pray. Lara saturated her heart and her mind with the promises in God's Word, praying "continually" — and we can do the same thing.[2] Set aside time each day when you and your spouse will commit to earnest prayer for your teen. If you are a single parent or if your spouse will not join you in prayer, ask God to give you another prayer partner. Take courage from

---

1. John 10:10. 2. 1 Thessalonians 5:17.

Jesus' words in Matthew 18:19–20: "If two of you on earth agree about anything you ask for, it will be done for you by my Father in heaven. For where two or three come together in my name, there am I with them."

Prayer Principle

No matter how far your teen strays,
God is always loving him, always pursuing him,
and always calling him back.

Love. So often, we think of love as a warm and fuzzy feeling, but more often than not, love is a decision. Paul could have been writing an advice column for parents of teens when he crafted his first letter to the Corinthian church. Love is many things, wrote Paul—patient, kind, not easily angered; it always protects, always trusts, always hopes, and always perseveres.[1] If we try to parent without love—establishing rules and enforcing discipline—we are setting ourselves up for trouble.

Prodigal teens can be tough to love. If we had to rely on our own strength, we'd be doomed. Thankfully, though, we are not alone. God has given us a beautiful example of unconditional love—sticking by our side and calling us back to him, no matter how many times we blow it—and as we pray for our teens, we can ask him to pour this same love into our hearts. God will never give up on our teens, and neither should we.

Because love, as 1 Corinthians 13:8 reminds us, *never* fails.

---

1. See 1 Corinthians 13:4–7.

Prayers You Can Use

Heavenly Father,

When _____ was a child, you loved him, Lord. You taught him to walk and led him with cords of human kindness and ties of love. Now, as he seems determined to turn from you, have compassion, dear Lord, and do not be angry. Put an end to his rebellious plans, and cause him to follow you. Bring him home again. HOSEA 11:1–11

Lift _____ out of the slimy pit she is in, out of the mud and mire. Give her a firm place to stand, and put a new song in her mouth—a hymn of praise to you. May all who seek to harm _____ be turned back in confusion and disgrace. PSALM 40:2–3, 14

Teach _____ to fear you and worship you and listen to your voice. Do not let him rebel against your commands, but cause him to follow you, so that all will be well in his life.

1 SAMUEL 12:14

Bring people into _____'s life who will gently instruct her. Grant her repentance leading to the knowledge of the truth, so that she will come to her senses and escape from the trap of the devil, who has taken her captive to do his will.

2 TIMOTHY 2:25–26

Today, let _____ listen to your voice. Do not let him harden his heart, rebelling against you and testing your patience, Lord. Do not be angry because of his stubbornness; instead, soften his heart and protect him from the deceitfulness of sin. Let him be faithful, putting his trust in you just as firmly as he did when he first believed.   HEBREWS 3:7–14

Save _____, and help her. Deliver her according to your great love. Give our family the help we need; with you, we will gain the victory as you trample our enemies.

PSALM 108:6, 12–13

Help me realize that _____ is a reward from you. You compare him to an arrow; help me point him straight toward you. Keep me mindful of my responsibility to contend with the enemies that want to tear our family down.

PSALM 127:3–5

When _____ wanders in the desert, lost and homeless, rescue her from her distress and lead her to a place of safety. When she sits in darkness and deepest gloom, rebelling against your word and scorning your counsel, lead her out and snap her chains. When she makes foolish decisions, heal her; when she heads off on her own, let her see your power in action. In the years to come, may we look at our family history and see your faithful love, precious Lord.

PSALM 107:4–24, 43

Cause _____ to grab hold of wisdom so that he will enjoy protection. Do not let him set foot on the path of the wicked or walk in the way of evildoers; instead, let him walk in the path of the righteous.   PROVERBS 4:6, 14

Let _____ put her hope in your unfailing love, knowing that with you is full redemption from every kind of sin.   PSALM 130:7 – 8

Call _____ back to you, and heal his wayward heart.   JEREMIAH 3:22

Thank you, Lord, for the riches of your kindness, tolerance, and patience. It is your kindness that leads us toward repentance.   ROMANS 2:4

Even as the shepherd rejoiced in the return of his lost sheep, and the woman when she found her lost coin, let us rejoice in your faithfulness when you bring _____ back to our home. Let the dead be made alive and the lost be found.   LUKE 15:1 – 10, 32

PART 4

PRAYING
for Your **TEEN'S**
VICTORY over
TEMPTATION

CHAPTER 18

Praying about Time Online

I will set before my eyes
no vile thing....
I will have nothing to do with evil.
PSALM 101:3–4

Last year, our school sponsored an Internet safety and awareness seminar for parents of teens. Among other things, we learned that our kids have a whole online vocabulary that they use to communicate their thoughts and emotions. LOL, for instance, means "laugh out loud." JK is "just kidding." POS is used by teens to alert their online friends that a parent is looking over their shoulder.

The other parents and I left the meeting armed with a packet of material that included the definitions for hundreds of these acronyms. Some of them were sexually suggestive (NIFOC means "nude in front of computer"); some were invitations (LMIRL is "let's meet in real life"); and some were just plain odd. Do you know what NALOPKT means? Next time you want to divulge something really juicy or personal over the Internet, start with NALOPKT. You'll be clueing your readers in that "not a lot of people know this, but ..."

A couple of weeks after the seminar, my friend Beth pulled up the text of an instant message session that her daughter Lexy had had with some friends the night before. Reading the letters ALJSLKAGHFSL, she consulted the dictionary portion of our packet. Nothing resembling that code was listed. Figuring that she stumbled onto some new lingo, she set about decoding the letters: *All lovers just say ... Any losers jump ship ... Apples leave juice stains ...*

Nothing made sense. Hating to admit defeat but knowing she needed help — what if Lexy was involved in something really sinister? — Beth asked her other daughter, Hannah, if she knew what the strange letters meant. "I know you girls don't like me snooping around on the computer," she said, "but I'm really worried about Lexy. What on earth could she be talking about?"

Hannah took one look at the computer screen and started to LOL. "Mom!" she cackled. "Those letters don't mean anything! That's just the sort of thing we type when we're frustrated, or when we don't know what to say. It's just random keys — like when you're talking to somebody and you say, 'Aaaarghh!'"

JSAKLGHS ... OIGLKSAJKLFH! No wonder we have a hard time keeping up with our teens!

It's been said that today's kids are Internet "natives," while parents are "immigrants." For many parents, the cyberworld represents unfamiliar — and ever-changing — territory, and it scares us. A recent poll revealed that computer use is the number one media concern for parents — a significant shift from a few years ago, when the television played the part of Family Enemy Number One.

It's a concern that is well founded. Studies show that nine out of ten children aged eight to sixteen have viewed pornography on the Internet—often unintentionally and usually while doing their homework. One in five kids has received a sexual solicitation online. And half of all teenage Internet users "frequently" communicate online with someone they've never met.[1]

Statistics like these make my toenails start to curl, but they don't even begin to address another Internet danger—namely, using computers to spread gossip, rumors, and vicious insults. In a phenomenon known as "cyberbullying," schoolyard confrontations often take a backseat to technological trashing, with entire websites being created to vote for, say, a school's "biggest slut, ugliest student, the most hated, and so on."[2] Lured by a false sense of anonymity, Internet users will often say and do things they would never consider in a face-to-face conversation—and every research site I checked while working on this chapter confirmed that cyberbullying has become commonplace among today's teens. While the percentage points vary slightly from study to study, the bottom line is that well over half of our kids are either dishing it out or taking it in every single day.

If you are a parent of a teen who has not (yet) flirted with Internet pornography, bullying, or other danger areas, count yourself blessed—and take another look at his or her computer. As I was working on this chapter, I lost count of how many parents I talked with who told me that they "just happened" to be walking by the home office when they noticed

1. Research available through ProtectKids.com (www.protectkids.com) and the Polly Klaas Foundation (www.pollyklass.org).

2. Keturah Gray, *How Mean Can Teens Be?* Last updated September 12, 2006. *ABC News: www.abcnews.go.com/Primetime/story?id=2421562&page=1* (November 16, 2006).

their son or daughter engaged in a questionable online conversation or logged on to an interactive website such as MySpace or Facebook without their parents' knowledge or approval. My own daughter Virginia was eleven or twelve years old when I found her pecking away at the keyboard, happily compiling information about herself — her school, her hobbies, her friends, and her picture — as she worked to create her own on-line "profile."

"It's OK, Mom," she said when I asked what she was doing. "I haven't mentioned my last name."

When I told her that all someone would have to do was to log on to the website where she had planned to post her information, get a copy of her school yearbook, and find her photo, and then simply look up her name in the telephone book to find out where she lived, Virginia looked as though she had been shot. I thanked God for giving me the opportunity to talk with her — and I shuddered to think how many other kids just like her log on to the Internet every day with a false sense of security and control.

My friend Lynnette has become an Internet watchdog of sorts, and she welcomes the opportunity to educate other parents about passwords, search engines, and particularly hazardous Internet sites. She wasn't always so "in the know." Once upon a time she was just like me — an Internet immigrant who thinks that successfully attaching a document to an email is a major coup. But all it took was one peek at her teenage son's computer screen to transform Lynnette from a mild-mannered mom into a porn-stopping pit bull...

"Hey, Kyle!" Lynnette called out to her son, who seemed focused on the computer in front of him. "Dinner is in about fifteen minutes—how's the homework coming?"

"Fine," Kyle mumbled. "OK."

Stepping back from the stove to where she had a clear view of the family's home office, Lynnette peered around to see what Kyle was working on. It didn't look much like homework; in fact, Lynnette was pretty sure that what she was seeing on the screen was the transcript of a lengthy instant messaging session.

"Kyle," she said, moving closer, "you know how I feel about IM-ing when you're supposed to be—*what is that?*"

There, on the screen, was a message from one of Kyle's friends—a kid he'd gotten to know at the Christian school he attended: *"I'm going to get to my science project after I download some porn."*

"He is going to download *porn?*" Lynnette had to read the message twice to be sure she was seeing it right.

"Come on, Mom," Kyle said. "Don't freak out. It's not that big of a deal—almost all the guys do it."

"Listen to me, Kyle," Lynnette said, forgetting all about the dinner she had been preparing. "Ever since you were a baby, I've prayed that you will be caught if you are doing anything wrong."

Kyle knew that was true—and usually, according to his calculations, he wound up getting nabbed within about twenty-four hours of any mischief making.

"And my goal," Lynnette continued, "is to keep you pure. Right now, nothing is more important to me than that. When you get married, or even when you're in a dating relationship, you don't want to be carrying around all these destructive immoral images in your mind."

"I think you're overreacting," Kyle said.

Lynnette knew that she had her work cut out for her. She also knew that, deep down, Kyle recognized that pornography was wrong—but she worried that the influence of his peers would crowd out anything that she or her husband tried to teach him. If she couldn't count on Kyle to look away from the computer screen or refuse to log on to some of the sites his friends recommended, she realized that she would have to stand guard on his behalf.

Lynnette googled "parental control programs." The search yielded a "Top 10" list, and she chose one that looked like it would work for what she needed. Next, she created a "white list" of sites that Kyle could visit, as well as a "black list" of those to which he would be denied access. She began compiling a notebook of passwords and codes, so that she would have ready access to any site Kyle visited or any program he ran. Finally, she purchased a program that provided a record of every single keystroke and of every screen that popped up—and how long it stayed on the monitor.

"You're invading my privacy!" Kyle protested.

"I'm protecting your purity," Lynnette replied.

The more Lynnette learned, the more vigilant she became. "It was kind of embarrassing," she laughs, thinking back to the long days of summer when Kyle would ask to hang out at a friend's house. "I would call up these moms I hardly knew and ask what sort of protection they had on their home computer. Some of them had no idea what I was talking about!"

If Lynnette had any doubts about the validity of her concerns, they disappeared with a single email that appeared in her mailbox. Thinking that it would add to her online savvy, she opened the mysterious file. "It was just some SPAM thing, but it was pretty hardcore stuff," she says, "and the image I saw is burned into my mind. Our kids may think they are just testing the waters when they go to one of those porn sites, but those are images they'll never be able to get rid of."

Prayer Principle

When you monitor your teen's Internet use,
you are not invading his privacy;
you are protecting his purity — and his future.

If you're like me, you might think that the market for Internet pornography is mostly lonely old men, perverts who sit alone in darkened apartments with a couple of beers and some leftover Chinese food in their refrigerators. Not so. The largest group of viewers of Internet porn is made up of kids, aged twelve to seventeen.[1]

Did you catch that? Internet pornography is a multibillion dollar industry, and their target market is our *teens!*

And, as Lynnette is all too aware, that doesn't bode well for the future. "Today's teens have been so overexposed," she says. "I cannot imagine what this crop of teenage boys will be like as husbands."

Yikes! As a mom of three teenage daughters, that certainly gets my attention. It's time to get proactive — and to pray!

---

1. Information available through www.ProtectKids.com.

Poised for Prayer

Lynnette's "let my kids get caught" prayer is, as I point out in the chapter called "Praying for Sin to Be Exposed," the most common prayer request I've encountered among parents of teens—and when it comes to Internet safety, it's a great place to start. Pray that your kids won't get away with *anything* that is hurtful or dangerous. Don't worry if you don't know the difference between a blog and a banana. God does. And he can protect our kids—even against those concerns or dangers that we don't know enough to name.

As you pray, remember the example that Nehemiah set. As he and his fellow Jews worked to rebuild the walls of Jerusalem, they faced intense opposition from their enemies, who plotted ways to stir up trouble and destroy the work. In response to this threat, Nehemiah did three things: he prayed, he posted a guard, and he came up with a plan to fight back.[1]

We can do these same things as we work to repel the Internet invasion. Let's pray—for our own teens and for their entire generation—using the Scriptures at the end of this chapter and our own heartfelt cries to the Lord. Our culture isn't all that different from that of the Israelites in the days when Jeremiah issued his warnings, and—like the mothers and fathers in his day—we should follow the prophet's charge to pour out our hearts "like water before the presence of the Lord" and lift up our hands to him for the lives of our children.[2]

Let's also post a guard. In his insightful book *"It's Only a Tattoo" and Other Myths Teens Believe*, Teen Mania founder Ron Luce offers some vital safeguards that we can bring into our homes:

---

1. You can read this story in Nehemiah 4.   2. Lamentations 2:19.

- Spend quality time together so that our kids aren't looking elsewhere to fill their need for family or community ties. We cannot let the computer, the television, or other media nudge relationships—with family members and with God—out of our lives.
- Bring the computer into a common area of the home. Computers in places like bedrooms—where no one is "watching"—can be an invitation to trouble. Be alert to danger signs, such as when a teen quickly exits a screen or closes his or her laptop when you walk into the room.
- Establish some rules for Internet use and monitor what our teens do—and whom they communicate with—when they are online. An Internet filter is essential; you can find some excellent choices using a Google search, as Lynnette did, or check out some of the sites Luce recommends, including www.afafilter.com, www.hedge.org, and christianbroadband.com.
- Model a "holy horror" toward pornography and a sincere, consistent respect for women and men. If we find that our teens are involved in pornography, our first response should be one of love. They need to know that we love them, but we hate what pornography will do to their minds and spirits, and that we will help them make a plan to guard against temptation in the future.

Our kids may think we are the strictest parents in the world, and we need to be prepared for the fact that we might not be very popular in their eyes, at least for the time being. But that's where the third part of Nehemiah's strategy can help.

In addition to praying and posting a guard, Nehemiah's plan called for unity among the Israelites and a willingness to fight together to keep the whole group safe. Nobody in his company was allowed to work alone; they used a buddy system — with each worker carrying a weapon along with his tools and building materials. At the first sign of an invasion, Nehemiah would have his own buddy sound the trumpet, and the Israelites would close ranks to repel the attackers.

That's how we need to do it. We need to look around in our churches, schools, and neighborhoods and build a community of parents who will work together to safeguard our kids. If you are like my friend Lynnette, you can help educate and equip other parents. Perhaps your youth pastor or the computer guru at your school would be willing to sponsor an informational event to let families know what they can do in their own homes.

Above all else, we can put Nehemiah's buddy system to work in our prayer lives. In Matthew 18:20, Jesus says that where two or three come together in his name, he is there with them. Here's the net effect: when we pray with a fellow believer, we invite the Lord into our prayer circle.

Let's sound the trumpet. God will not fail to come to our rescue.

Prayers You Can Use

Heavenly Father,

Cause _____ to keep his eyes focused on you, knowing that you are the only one who can keep him from being ensnared by evil. Let integrity and uprightness protect him as he puts his hope in you. Psalm 25:15, 21.

Let _____ be careful to lead a blameless life. Strengthen her resolve so that she will not be tempted to look at anything vile or vulgar. Cause her to reject perverse ideas, stay away from evil, and refuse to tolerate any kind of slander— whether it is done face-to-face, over the telephone, or online. Psalm 101:2–4

Let no unwholesome words or pictures have a place on _____'s computer screen. Instead, let all that he communicates be helpful for building up other people according to their needs, so that his use of technology would be a benefit to all. Ephesians 4:29

Guard _____'s heart and mind so that she will not spend her time gossiping, getting into other people's business, and saying things online that she would never dream of saying in front of anyone. 1 Timothy 5:13

Let _____ have nothing to do with the fruitless deeds of darkness, and help him to realize that it is shameful to even talk about these things, let alone participate in them. If he is involved in anything dark or evil, expose his thoughts and actions and draw him back into the light of your love.
EPHESIANS 5:11 – 13

If _____ is trying to hide anything that offends you, please search it out—and then lead her along the path of everlasting life.
PSALM 139:11, 24

You see all that _____ does—every website he visits, every chat room he enters, and every online path he takes. Teach him that when he deliberately chooses to sin, he will find himself held captive. Protect him, Lord, so that he will not die for his lack of self-control or be lost because of his incredible folly.
PROVERBS 5:21 – 23

As _____ uses the Internet, remind her that she is to imitate you by living a life of love. Cause her to reject anything that bears even a hint of sexual immorality, obscenity, foolish talk, or of any kind of impurity, knowing that these things are not right for her.
EPHESIANS 5:3 – 4

Protect _____ by the power of your name. As he lives and studies and interacts with his friends in a world that does not know you, protect him from the evil one, and sanctify him by your truth.   JOHN 17:11, 15 – 18

Help _____ to be self-controlled and alert to the traps and dangers represented via the Internet. Let her be on guard against Satan and his schemes, and protect her so that no harm can come near her.   1 PETER 5:8; PSALM 91:10

Open my eyes and teach me, Lord, so that I will be equipped to set limits and establish rules for Internet use in our house. Give me wisdom, and cause my teens to listen to my instruction and not forsake my teaching in this important area.
          PROVERBS 1:8

CHAPTER 19

Praying for Protection from Drinking

Wine is a mocker and beer a brawler;
whoever is led astray by them is not wise.

PROVERBS 20:1

I went to college at the University of Virginia. At the time, the school had an abysmal football program, a top academic rating, and a reputation for throwing some of the nation's best (or worst, depending on your perspective) cocktail parties. The local grocery store — part of a national chain — welcomed students back to school every year by stacking cases of beer into towering pyramids, and it prided itself on selling more of the stuff than any other store in the country.

I lived with a couple of brainiacs named Susan and Barbie. Susan, I discovered, had been an SAT whiz kid with a vocabulary the size of Texas, and in an effort to upgrade our verbal repertoire as we discussed the university's party scene, she began posting useful words on the walls of our apartment. "Obstreperous," I learned, could be employed to describe behavior that was marked by unruly or aggressive noisiness. "Temerarious" signaled a tendency to be rash, reckless, or daring. And "corybantic"—which quickly became a household favorite, in light of some of the fraternity dances we attended—meant "wild" and "frenzied."

In addition to being incredibly smart, Susan and Barbie were deeply committed Christians. When we realized how much attention our "vocabulary in the foyer" program garnered among our friends, we branched out into Scripture memory, taping index cards to the walls of our kitchen. One card that never failed to draw comments was Proverbs 23:29–35:

Who has woe? Who has sorrow?
     Who has strife? Who has complaints?
     Who has needless bruises? Who has bloodshot eyes?
Those who linger over wine,
     who go to sample bowls of mixed wine.
Do not gaze at wine when it is red,
     when it sparkles in the cup,
     when it goes down smoothly!
In the end it bites like a snake
     and poisons like a viper.
Your eyes will see strange sights,
     and your mind imagine confusing things.
You will be like one sleeping on the high seas,
     lying on top of the rigging.
"They hit me," you will say, "but I'm not hurt!
     They beat me, but I don't feel it!
When will I wake up
     so I can find another drink?"

"*That's* not in the Bible!" a visitor would protest.

"Oh, yes it is!" we'd crow, opening our Bibles to prove ourselves right—and cementing our status as total nerds.

Back then, we laughed at the drunks—and marveled when they managed to show up for class the next day. Now that I have teens, and every weekend seems to bring another story about some kid who passed out in the bathroom, alcohol isn't so funny. The fact that there are plenty of parents who facilitate underage drinking—"*someone* needs to teach these kids to drink responsibly before they go off to college"—only makes the situation worse. I thought things might improve after a high-profile group of athletes in our town were caught drinking—with photographic proof—and had to forfeit part of their season, but I was wrong. "Did the kids learn a lesson?" I asked one parent. "Oh, yes," she answered. "They learned not to have their picture taken with a beer in their hand."

I wish I could say that teenage alcohol use was a public school problem or a private school problem or a problem in households where parents drink—or where they don't. The truth, as one of my teacher-friends lamented the other day, is that alcohol is *everywhere*. What, then, are we parents supposed to do?

At the end of this chapter, you'll find plenty of prayer verses designed to petition God to protect your teen from alcohol use and help him (or her) resist peer pressure to drink. For those of you who already find yourself mired in the world I described earlier—one where kids drink, parents wink, and even the most well-intentioned teen can find himself or herself in a bad spot with alcohol—I want to encourage you to take a deep breath and remember that, even though he may allow a season of destruction, God's ultimate aim is redemption.

Most of the stories I've shared in this book came from praying moms—either my friends or women I've met via the Internet. The other night, though, my husband, Robbie, and I had dinner with a husband and his wife and, when they heard I was working on a book about praying for teens, here's what this *dad* had to say ...

As a young child, Roger had seen—firsthand—the devastating impact that alcohol could have on a family. His uncle often came home drunk and in a fit of rage would hurl furniture around the room, sometimes smashing the windows. Seeking refuge anyplace he could, Roger resolved that alcohol would *never* be part of his life—or his family's.

Roger grew up, got married, and had two sons—Samuel, the serious older brother, and Danny, the free-spirited thrill seeker who never seemed to get enough of things like skiing, surfing, and skydiving. Danny was a good boy, and when he got his driver's license, Roger and his wife, Lynn, bought him his dream car—a used Jeep with oversized tires. When he'd pull into the driveway and flash one of his 100-watt smiles, Lynn felt as though her heart might melt.

Midway through his high school career, though, Danny began to change. He still came to church, and he exhibited a tenderness and compassion not often seen in teenage boys, but like the sunshine slipping behind the clouds, his joy sometimes turned into sullenness. Was that normal for a teen? Roger wasn't sure.

Then, too, there was the question of Danny's friends. He had always been drawn to kids who shared his passion for adventure, and while Roger reckoned that they were a bit of a maverick crowd, he didn't see any real danger in letting Danny pal around with the group. At least not until he and Lynn came home from church late on a Friday night.

The telephone was ringing as they entered the house. "Hello?" Roger said.

"Is this Mr. _____?" came a voice he did not recognize. Who would be calling at eleven o'clock on a Friday night?

"Is Danny your son?" the voice persisted.

"Yes, he is. Is everything all right? Who is this?"

The caller identified himself as a police officer. "Danny's OK," he said, "but we found him in a section of woods near the high school. He was lying facedown. He is completely intoxicated."

"He's drunk?" Roger asked. "Are you sure?"

"Oh, yes. He kept mumbling, 'Dad, Dad.' We finally got him to say your name so that we could call you. Can you come over to the jail and get him? We'd rather not lock him up for the night. He's in pretty bad shape."

"We'll be right there."

Roger and Lynn drove to the jail, not saying a word. In Roger's mind, he replayed a multitude of scenes from Danny's life—joyous moments that stood in stark contrast to the idea of a boy lying drunk in the bushes. He wondered what he would discover when they got to the jail.

They found Danny slumped on the floor, glassy-eyed and with slobber flowing out of his mouth. His face had been cut, and Roger noticed Danny's glasses lying smashed on the floor beside him. Torn between love for his son and a raging anger, Roger asked the officer to help him lift Danny into the car.

"I'm sorry, Dad," Danny mumbled, as the two men maneuvered his limp body into the backseat of the car. "I'm so sorry."

Roger climbed in next to his boy. As Lynn pulled the car away from the curb, Danny vomited on his father's chest. With the weight of his son's head on his shoulder, Roger recalled the words he had said a thousand times before, ever since Danny had learned to talk: "Daddy loves you, Son. No matter what, Daddy will always love you."

Now that push had come to shove, he hoped he would make good on his promise.

Roger and Lynn put Danny into bed. He was still lying there the next afternoon, when Roger came up and sat beside him.

"Daddy loves you, Son."

Danny was quiet, but Roger knew that he was awake. "Do you know what happened last night?"

Danny opened his eyes just a crack. "No, Dad," he whispered.

"Well, you apparently had a lot to drink either during or after the football game. Your buddies let you out of their car and left you to wander in the woods. A policeman found you, and called Mom and me."

"Danny," Roger continued, "do you remember what I've always said — that no matter what happens, I will always love you?"

"Yes, Dad."

"Well, it's true. So let's put this behind us, OK?"

"OK."

"OK, then." Roger paused for a moment, not entirely certain what to say next. "So — can we fix you some soup?"

Poised for Prayer

When Roger told me his story, he added the fact that Danny is now married, and he and his wife are expecting their first child, a boy. Both excited and nervous about becoming a dad, Danny feels sure about at least one aspect of his parenting style: "No matter what," he says, "my boy is going to know that his daddy loves him."

If you are taking the time to read this book, my guess is that you love your child, too. If you suspect that alcohol use is becoming a serious problem, seek pastoral or professional help right away. Get to know your teen's friends, and don't be afraid to do a little investigative parenting, spot-checking things like text messages and taking the time to call and see whether so-and-so's parents really are home. "It's not snooping," a counselor friend once told me. "It's called *surveillance*— and as parents, it's our job."

Listening to Roger's tale, I couldn't help but think of Jesus' parable of the prodigal son, found in Luke 15. When that boy—the younger son—took his inheritance early and then squandered the whole wad in wild living, it did absolutely nothing to change his father's love. Dirt-poor and starving, the boy finally decided to go home, intending to ask his father to take him back—not as a son but as one of the hired men on the farm. As Jesus tells the story, the father saw his son when he was still a long way off. Dropping everything, he gathered up his robes and ran—ran!—to meet his boy, throwing his arms open wide to welcome his lost son home.

Coming as this parable does on the heels of two others— that of the lost sheep and then the lost coin—I am convinced that the father never stopped loving his son, nor did he ever stop looking for him to return. As parents, we need to be equally faithful in our love, equally diligent in our prayers, and equally expectant in our attitude as we wait for God to move.

Prayer Principle

As parents, we must be faithful in love,
diligent in prayer, and expectant in attitude as we
wait for God to work in our teen's life.

When we catch our kids doing something wrong—whether they break a curfew, squander their money, or turn up drunk in the bushes—I want to pray that we will respond as beautifully as Roger did and with as much love, compassion, and grace as the father in Luke 15. I want to run—not walk—to embrace my wayward teens (even if they have to undergo some discipline in the process), banishing any doubt that, no matter what has happened, I am still crazy in love with them.

Just like my heavenly daddy is still crazy in love with foolish, mistake-prone, wayward-walking me.

Prayers You Can Use

Heavenly Father,

Let _____ thirst for a drink from your river of delights rather than for anything that alcohol offers.   PSALM 36:8

Cause _____ to be decent and true in all that he does, so that everyone can approve of his behavior. Do not let him participate in wild parties or getting drunk, or in fighting and jealousy. Instead, let the Lord Jesus Christ take control of his life, so that he will not spend time thinking of ways to indulge his evil desires.   ROMANS 13:13–14

Don't let _____ be drunk with alcohol, which will ruin her life, but fill her instead with your Holy Spirit so that he can control her life.   EPHESIANS 5:18

Show _____ that whatever he chooses to obey [his peers, his craving for alcohol, his desire for popularity] will become his master. Show him that if he chooses to obey sin, it will lead to death — but that if he decides to obey you, Lord, he will receive your approval.   ROMANS 6:16

Help _____ to live by the Spirit so that she will not want to gratify the desires of her sinful nature. Instead of being filled with things like debauchery or drunkenness, fill her with the fruit of the Spirit, that she might know that she belongs to Jesus Christ and has crucified her sinful nature with its passions and desires. GALATIANS 5:19–25

Give _____ an eagerness to do your will, even when his friends say evil things about him because he refuses to join in their drunkenness, wild parties, or other wickedness.

1 PETER 4:2–4

Help _____ to be self-controlled and alert, knowing that Satan is her enemy and that he is on the prowl and looking for someone to devour. When Satan tries to use things like alcohol or peer pressure to cause _____ to stumble, help her to stand firm and resist his evil schemes. Remind her that she stands with godly teens all over the world who face similar temptations, persecution, and suffering.

1 PETER 5:8–10

Cause _____ to listen to your commands and become wise. Do not let him join those who drink too much alcohol or gorge themselves on meat, for drunkards and gluttons become poor, and drowsiness clothes them in rags.

PROVERBS 23:19–21

When _____ is tempted by alcohol or peer pressure, do not let her be tempted beyond what she can bear. Open her eyes so that she can see the way out, and help her to stand firm.   1 CORINTHIANS 10:13

Cause _____ to listen to my teaching and instruction. If his friends try to entice him with alcohol, strengthen his resolve so that he will not give in to them. When they say, "Come and join us," give him the courage to stay far away from their paths.   PROVERBS 1:8, 10, 15

Thank you for your grace, which teaches _____ to say "No" to ungodliness and worldly passions and to live an upright and godly life among her peers.   TITUS 2:11–12

Prompt _____ to live a life of moral excellence, which leads to knowing you better, which leads to self-control—so that ultimately he will be productive and useful.

2 PETER 1:5–8

When the time comes for me to discipline _____, help her not to become discouraged. Help me to show her how much I love her and that, even as you discipline those you love, my correction is a sign that I delight in her.

PROVERBS 3:11–12

CHAPTER 20

Praying for Sexual Purity

*Do you not know that your body
is a temple of the Holy Spirit, who is in you,
whom you have received from God?
You are not your own; you were bought at a price.
Therefore honor God with your body.*

1 CORINTHIANS 6:19–20

As I was pulling together some research for this book, I had the opportunity to talk to a group of teenage girls—high school sophomores, juniors, and seniors—about some of the lies girls believe. Specifically, we looked at the deceptions and twisted truths that girls (and plenty of women) buy in to when it comes to their bodies. We covered such things as *appearance* ("the more attractive you are, the better you are"), *reputation* ("nobody will judge you, think less of you, or talk about you if you mess around"), *self-image* ("the faster you are, the more guys will like you and the more you will like yourself"), and *sex* ("it's OK as long as you love the person").

My daughter Hillary was part of the mix. She didn't say much, and I worried that she might be sitting there hating life, wishing she could be anyplace other than in a room full of mostly older girls listening to her mother talk about things

239

like sex. She told me afterward that she had, in fact, wondered about how the evening would go — but her fears (and mine) were allayed by the group's very positive response. Girls opened up about their thoughts and concerns about all manner of related subjects. "This is the kind of thing all of us need to hear, but nobody ever talks about it," one girl said. "Yeah," another chimed in, "you're lucky, Hillary, that your mom can talk about this stuff."

Truth be told, I *don't* talk to Hillary — or any of my kids — all that much when it comes to squirmy subjects like sex. From the very first conversations about puberty — when our preteens are apt to cover their ears and say, "Yuck!" — to the more specific questions about such things as "how far is too far?" you'd be hard pressed to find a parent (or a kid!) who feels totally comfortable with this subject, and I'm no different. I find it far easier to give a "Sex Talk" to a group of fifty middle schoolers than to have a heart-to-heart with one of my own teens about what they ought to be doing — or not doing — with their bodies.

If parents are uncomfortable talking about sex, it's a safe bet that we aren't doing a whole lot of proactive praying about it either. If you picked up this book and flipped straight to this chapter, my guess is that you suspect — or know — that your teen has already gone farther down the road than you would like, and you're looking for a way to pray him or her out of a bad situation. (That's OK, by the way. The Bible is full of "Rescue me!" prayers — and frankly, the worse things look, the brighter God shines. Like a candle in the darkness, God's majesty and power can often be seen most clearly against a backdrop of despair.)

Maybe, like many Christian parents, you thought that your teen's relationship with Christ would offer a measure of purity protection. Maybe you thought that your church's youth group leader would somehow convince your son to set some sexual boundaries—and honor them. Maybe you thought your daughter was safe because she hangs out with such a "nice" crowd.

Or maybe, like the mom in this story, you simply thought "it" could never happen in your family ...

"Ninety percent of families have trouble with their teens and they don't even know about it."

Clare turned to her friend and prayer partner Nancy, who sat in the passenger seat as the two women made their way toward a prayer leaders' retreat sponsored by Moms in Prayer. "Did you hear that?" she asked.

Nancy nodded. The two had been listening to a Christian radio broadcast during the drive, and they were getting an earful of parenting advice.

"Ninety percent!" Clare repeated. "I feel *so* sorry for those people."

Clare drove on, but her thoughts were far from the highway. She knew that her fourteen-year-old son, Troy, could be mischievous at times, but as she listened to the harrowing tales of other people's teens, she counted her blessings. Troy was an only child, and he attended a Christian school; and Clare pretty much always knew what was going on in his life. Thinking about all those unfortunate parents—that poor 90 percent! —she was glad she didn't have to worry about her son.

At the retreat, Clare found herself soaking up biblical teaching on all manner of subjects, including a session on how to pray for your teen's sexual purity. When the speaker offered a five-page prayer handout on the subject, Clare eagerly took a copy. It looked like a valuable tool — and who knew? Maybe one of the moms in her prayer group back home would need it.

Clare also found herself paired with a woman named Cindy, a mother whose two sons were about the same age as Troy. On their last day together, Cindy prayed for Clare, using the words of Isaiah 58:11 (NASB): "Father God," she prayed, "continually guide Clare and satisfy her desire in scorched places. Give strength to her bones, and let her be like a watered garden, like a spring whose waters do not fail."

Clare nodded her assent, agreeing with Cindy's words. But her prayer partner wasn't finished. "Lord, give strength to Clare's *tired* and *weary* bones. Give her *perseverance* during the times of scorching."

As Cindy continued to pray, zeroing in on Clare's apparent weariness and her need for strength, Clare found herself pulling back. "Hold on a minute!" she thought to herself. "I only have one son — and he's a pretty good boy. I mean, thanks for the prayers and all — but honestly, my life is just not that hard!"

Still wondering what Cindy could have meant with all of her "scorching" prayers, Clare pulled into her driveway after the retreat. She was on top of the world — spiritually renewed and ready to pray for her family with a fresh enthusiasm. Troy came out to help carry her bags, but was uncharacteristically silent. "What's up?" Clare asked.

"Nothing," Troy mumbled.

"Nothing" turned out to be something that left Clare reeling. While she was gone, Troy had been caught masturbating in a thicket near their home, along with a younger boy from his school. Like many praying parents, Clare had often asked God to let her son get caught if he was plotting, or doing, anything wrong—but never in her wildest dreams could she have imagined something like this. It had to be some sort of a sick mistake.

"Boys will be boys," Clare's husband said when she asked him about what had happened. She knew that Bill was upset and that he was just trying to comfort her, but his words rang hollow—particularly given the five-page handout on sexual purity that she still had in her purse. All of those verses about honoring God with our bodies did not add up to anything that could endorse the picture of two boys masturbating in the bushes!

Clare was crushed. She felt uncertain and alone, and she wondered where she had gone wrong in raising her son. The other boy's mother—a neighbor and fellow Christian—had been the one to catch the boys, and she blamed Troy for what had happened. She didn't seem inclined to discuss the matter, let alone forgive anyone—and Clare found herself wondering whether she would be able to forgive Troy either. The words from Cindy's prayer echoed in her mind. Suddenly she knew why the woman had felt led to pray all that stuff about needing strength.

In the days that followed, it seemed that Clare's only comfort came from the Lord. His gentle whisper pierced her heart: "Haven't *I* forgiven *you?*" A lifetime of stupid mistakes flooded Clare's mind, and she realized that what Troy needed, more than anything else, were mercy and unconditional love. He *knew* that what he had done was wrong; now, Clare realized, the important thing was getting him back on the right track. Thankful that at least the lines of communication were open, she and Bill began to pray for Troy's healing, and that he would find acceptance from them—and, more importantly, from God.

Over time, several factors contributed to Troy's spiritual and emotional restoration. "God is so creative in the way he has worked in Troy's life," Clare told me. "For example, our city hosted a Pure Excitement rally.[1] Troy heard Joe White [author of a book called *Pure Excitement*] speak, and now all he can talk about is waiting until he gets married before he even kisses a girl!"

"Ultimately," Clare went on, "the things that Satan planned for Troy's ruin and defeat are the things that God used for his good. Our neighbors still won't talk to Troy—but even that is something that God is using to build his character and to teach us about forgiveness. We are still working our way through everything, but God has graciously allowed us to see how powerfully he can work, even in the midst of a very bad situation."

Prayer Principle

God's majesty and power can often be seen most clearly against a backdrop of despair.

---

1. Pure Excitement is a high-energy one-night event designed to show teens God's plan for sexual purity. For more information, please see the appendix in the back of this book.

Poised for Prayer

Like many Christian parents, I have a hefty collection of parenting books, a fair number of which deal specifically with teens. When it comes to sexual purity, all of the "experts" agree: it's best to talk about sex and dating as soon as possible — *before* your kids start to date. From a biblical perspective, two principles stand out: first, we need to learn to control our bodies in a way that is holy and honorable (1 Thessalonians 4:4), and second, because our bodies serve as a temple for the Holy Spirit, we should honor God in the way that we use them (1 Corinthians 6:19 – 20). These parallel concepts — control and honor — can be a springboard for discussion as well as prayer, and they can help you and your teen establish physical limits that will not bring dishonor to God.

But what about kids who have already crossed those lines? What if you're reading this chapter, knowing that your son or daughter has experimented with sex at some level? (I say "at some level" because, despite what we might want to believe, going "all the way" is not the only thing on God's "Don't" list. As Solomon wrote in his Song of Songs, we are not to "arouse or awaken love" prematurely[1] — and I'm not telling you anything you don't know when I say that there are plenty of ways outside of intercourse to stimulate or arouse our passions.)

If that's you — if you are a parent who wants to pray your teen out of an ongoing sexual relationship, or if you want God to heal the wounds from mistakes made in the past — then I can't tell you how glad I am that you picked up this book. God is a God of hope. He is in the redemption business. He heals

---

1. Song of Songs 2:7.

hearts and changes lives every day, and he can do it for you. More to the point, he can do it for your teen.

Start by thanking God that you know where you stand. If you know that your teen is having or has had a sexual relationship — either because he has told you voluntarily or because he has been caught — then the lines of communication are open. Armed with knowledge, you have an opportunity to talk about what is going on, to make a plan for the future, and — most important of all — to pray specifically and effectively for your child.

I'm sure that professional counselors have much more to offer on this subject, but I see a few key Scriptures that are loaded with wisdom. Galatians 6:1 (NLT) reads, "If another believer is overcome by some sin, you who are godly should gently and humbly help that person back onto the right path." As parents, we need to reassure our teens that we love them and that God does too. Satan would love to use this time to drive a wedge between your teen and God, making him feel worthless and ashamed, but Romans 8:38 – 39 says that nothing — *nothing!* — can separate him from God's love.

If your teen is open to the idea of restoration, don't miss the opportunity to present the concept of "secondary virginity" — the newness in Christ that is available to those who want to turn away from sin and receive forgiveness for past mistakes. After King David committed adultery with Bathsheba, he cried out to God for mercy. "Create in me a clean heart," he prayed. "Restore to me again the joy of your salvation, and make me willing to obey you."[1] The same God who gave David a new start can likewise cleanse and restore your teen.

---

1. Psalm 51:10 – 12 NLT.

God *loves* your daughter. Nobody—not her girlfriends, not her boyfriend, not even you, her mom or dad—spends more time thinking about her than God does. I love the way God describes his infatuation in Psalm 45:11: "The king is enthralled by your beauty; honor him, for he is your lord." The Almighty God of the universe is head over heels for your girl—and his heart's desire is that she honor him.

God *adores* your son. He knows his thoughts, his actions, his past, and his future. He wants the very best for his life—including a clean body and mind—and in Psalm 119:9, he offers a surefire strategy for success: "How can a young man keep his way pure? By living according to your word."

God's word holds the key to victory. As we pray for our teens' sexual purity, we can go to God in the same way Abraham did—against a backdrop of despair. "Against all hope," the Bible says, Abraham "did not waver through unbelief ..., but was strengthened in his faith and gave glory to God, being fully persuaded that God had the power to do what he had promised."[1]

Be fully persuaded. God has the power to protect, encourage, redeem, and transform your teen's life.

---

1. Romans 4:18, 20–21.

Prayers You Can Use

Heavenly Father,

You are the God who gives life to the dead and calls into being things that were not. Remind _____ that, when he trusts in you, his transgressions are forgiven and his sin will never be counted against him.

ROMANS 4:5 – 8, 17

Do not let sin reign in _____ body so that she obeys its evil desires. Do not allow her to use the parts of her body as instruments of wickedness, but prompt her to offer her body to you as an instrument of righteousness.

ROMANS 6:12 – 13

Create in _____ a pure heart, and renew a steadfast spirit within him. Give him joy and a spirit that is willing to obey you.

PSALM 51:10 – 12

Equip _____ to control her body and live in holiness and honor — not in passionate lust like the example so often set by people who do not know you.

1 THESSALONIANS 4:4 – 5

Teach _____ how to take every one of his thoughts captive and make it obedient to Christ.

2 CORINTHIANS 10:5

As _____ enters into romantic relationships, remind her that, above all else, she must guard her heart, for it affects everything she does. PROVERBS 4:23

Show _____ that his body was not made for sexual immorality but for you. Remind him how much you care about his body, because it belongs to you. Cause him to run away from sexual sin, knowing that no other sin so clearly affects his body—which is the temple of the Holy Spirit.

1 CORINTHIANS 6:13, 18–19

If _____ thinks that she is standing strong, remind her to be careful, lest she fall into sin. Keep the temptations in her life from becoming so strong that she cannot stand up against them. When she is tempted, show her your way out.

1 CORINTHIANS 10:12–13

Surround _____ with people who will be good examples for his life—men who are temperate, worthy of respect, self-controlled, strong in their faith, and filled with love and patience. In all that _____ does, let his conduct be marked by integrity, so that no one will have anything bad to say about him. TITUS 2:2, 6–8

Keep _____'s heart from growing hard. Keep her sensitive to your Holy Spirit, so that she will not want to give herself over to sensuality or indulge in any kind of impurity.
                                             EPHESIANS 4:18 – 19

In _____'s life, put to death all those things that belong to his earthly nature: sexual immorality, impurity, lust, evil desires, and greed, which is idolatry.   COLOSSIANS 3:5

Protect _____ from evildoers and anyone who would conspire against her.   PSALM 59:2

Keep _____'s heart from being drawn to evil; protect him from the snares and traps set by evildoers.
                                             PSALM 141:4, 9

When a deceitful man speaks charming words to _____, do not let her believe him.   PROVERBS 26:24 – 25

CHAPTER 21

Praying about Choice of Music

Among you [in your music] there must be not even a hint of sexual immorality, or of any kind of impurity, or of greed....
Nor should there be obscenity, foolish talk or coarse joking, which are out of place, but rather thanksgiving....

    Sing and make music in your heart to the Lord, always giving thanks to God the Father for everything, in the name of the Lord Jesus Christ.

EPHESIANS 5:3 – 4, 19B – 20

Lisa is one of my favorite prayer partners. She is also one of the coolest moms I know. She loves surfing, running, and watching professional sports. God knew what he was doing when he gave Lisa and her equally fun husband two boys to raise!

Lisa's oldest son, Michael, is the same age as Hillary. When he got his learner's permit, I could pray for his safety with conviction, knowing that Hillary was also behind the wheel. When Hillary tried out for her school's lacrosse team, Lisa was right there with me—the boys' tryouts were taking place at the same time. And when Michael and some of his buddies got together to form a band, I could empathize with Lisa's concerns. Although Hillary runs the soundboard for one of the worship bands at our church, her taste in music isn't always all that "churchy." Maybe there's a Christian message in some of that alternative stuff, but if so, I haven't heard it.

Which is, in itself, part of the problem. If we don't understand—or even like—the music our kids listen to, it can be tough to talk about it in a meaningful way. Any attempt to influence their choices is apt to be seen as old-fashioned or, as one briefly popular teen song put it, "so yesterday." How can we bridge the divide?

I was mulling this over in my mind one day when Lisa shared the following story. Reading it, you are going to think I'm making it up. I swear I'm not. As cheesy as it sounds, this really happened ...

Lisa's eyes were on the road, but she could sense her sixteen-year-old son's mocking attitude as she turned up the volume on her car radio. She loved contemporary Christian music, and she knew the words to almost every song her favorite station played. She was well aware that her kids preferred rock and jazz, but on days like today, when she was in the driver's seat, she kept the dial tuned to what she called "the good stuff."

"Aw, Mom," Michael groaned, "Don't you get enough of this kind of music on Sundays? You are way too into church. Can't we just listen to normal music, like normal people do?"

Lisa pulled into a parking spot, turning to smile at her son. "When you drive, you can listen to what you want. Now come on—let's get that hair cut. With the way it looks right now, I can't even tell if you *are* a normal person."

Walking into the salon, Lisa recalled a verse she had prayed earlier with her weekly Moms in Prayer group: "Lord, give Michael knowledge and insight so that he can discern what is best and be pure and blameless" (Philippians 1:9 – 10). Thinking of these words, she breathed a silent prayer for his taste in music. She looked up as their favorite hairdresser, Jean Marie, approached.

"Hey, Michael," Jean Marie teased. "Looks like you've been saving your hair up for me!"

"Yeah, I guess it's been a while," Michael said dryly. Jean Marie, Lisa knew, had a way of getting Michael to part with his hair and be happy about it — and looking at the pretty hairdresser, dressed in jeans and a T-shirt that showed her twenty-something figure to good advantage, Lisa had to admit that a teenage boy would have to be blind to not want to get his hair cut by her.

"So are you still playing guitar with that band?" Jean Marie asked, as she combed Michael's hair.

"Yeah," Michael replied.

"Do you play any Christian rock?"

Lisa's ears perked up. Could it be that this goddess of a hairdresser liked Christian music?

"Christian rock?" Michael scoffed. "There's no such thing. That's an oxymoron!"

"No way!" Jean Marie countered, snipping away. "You don't have to get in the *gutter* to rock out and enjoy some good music. You can rock out to the Spirit!" Michael didn't say anything, and Lisa wondered what he was thinking. But Jean Marie wasn't finished. "You know," she added, "I think there's nothing sexier than a man who loves Jesus."

Lisa nearly dropped the magazine she was holding. Michael, however, did not flinch—which, Lisa realized, was a good thing. Jean Marie's scissors did not look very forgiving.

"What makes you find Christian guys so appealing?" Lisa prompted, hoping that Michael was listening as closely as she was.

"Well," Jean Marie began, "they have an inner confidence—the kind that comes from the heart. It's so much more attractive than the insecurity or outward arrogance that so many guys have. When a man knows who he is in Christ, it shows in the way he treats people, in the things he does, and in the things he says. He has a genuine confidence—and girls like that."

Lisa turned her head so that Michael wouldn't see her smile. How very like God to put a beautiful young woman smack-dab in front of her son to deliver a message in a way no mother ever could. And the best part, Lisa thought to herself, was that since Michael's hair was two inches shorter on one side than on the other, he couldn't just get up and walk away!

Prayer Principle

Ask God to bring people into your teen's life
who can teach the lessons
he or she may not want to hear from you.

As a mother of teens whose musical preferences are often jaw-droppingly different from my own, I can relate to Lisa's desire to see her kids start listening to "the good stuff." I, too, want my kids to have discernment when it comes to choosing which lyrics, melodies, and rhythms they'll invite into their minds. We cannot underestimate the power that music has to shape attitudes, belief systems, and even behavior.

We bought one of our daughters an iPod for Christmas one year. I like to think of myself as one of those clued-in and involved parents, but there are a number of areas—including sports and music—in which my grasp of what's what leaves more than a lot to be desired. Every time Christmas or a kid's birthday rolls around, I thank God for giving me a husband who actually likes to shop for things like soccer cleats and stereo speakers.

Robbie is also our resident computer guru, and since he—unlike me—knows the lyrics to songs written after, say, 1980, I figured he would monitor the stuff that our girl downloaded and keep tabs on her playlist.

He did, but not right away—and not before both of us noticed a marked downturn in her countenance. Now, we're no strangers to teenage moods, but after about two weeks of living with Grumpy, we began to wonder if there was a connection between our daughter's sullenness and the wires that seemed to be permanently attached to her ears. Robbie asked her to hand over the iPod.

Sure enough, there were a handful of songs—several that were very popular among her classmates—that had some pretty negative messages. When Robbie shared his concerns, our daughter (thank you, God!) agreed to delete the offensive songs. Almost overnight, it seemed as though the sunshine came out in our family again.

Coincidence? Maybe. But maybe not.

Poised for Prayer

My grandmother used to threaten to throw her shoe through the television set, and every time I walked past her with my Sony Walkman, she would shake her head and mutter something that, thanks to my headphones, I couldn't hear. I thought she was a little bit nuts, but now that I'm a parent, I want to go knock on her grave and say, "I see what you mean!"

That being said, I know that throwing shoes and muttering at my kids isn't going to solve anything. Galatians 5:17 (NLT) says that the Holy Spirit "gives us desires that are opposite from what the sinful nature desires. These two forces are constantly fighting each other, and your choices are never free from this conflict." As my kids make choices about what to listen to, I want to teach them to spot the difference between the bad and the good—and pray that they choose the latter.

I'm sure that volumes could be written on this subject, but my litmus test for music is fairly simple: *Does the music glorify God—or does it put the spotlight on self?* Put another way, *Does the music promote pure and noble thoughts—or does it encourage sensuality, anger, materialism, physical pleasure, or other self-centered cravings?*

Talk with your teen about the songs he likes. Find out what's on his playlist. Teach him to spot the messages that songs promote, and give him a litmus test he can use. You may find yourself talking to a wall—my grandmother certainly did—but that's OK. In a world where our kids have instant access to every kind of music via iPods, computers, and even things like sunglasses with built-in MP3 players, we will never be able to monitor or filter everything they hear. But let's not start throwing shoes.

Instead, let's ask God to be the Master Conductor, tuning our kids' ears and opening their hearts to the music and the messages he wants them to hear. And as we pray for our teens in this very influential area, let's remember the words Moses sang after the Israelites had escaped through the Red Sea: "I will sing to the LORD, for he has triumphed gloriously .... The LORD is my strength and my song; he has become my victory" (Exodus 15:2–3 NLT).

God is sovereign over the world of music. And he—the God who created our teens' hearts, minds, and ears—is our victory song.

Prayers You Can Use

Heavenly Father,

As _____ listens to or plays music, cause him to realize that whatever he does should be done for your glory, Lord.

1 CORINTHIANS 10:31

Draw _____ into true fellowship with you, teaching her to listen to music that brings light instead of darkness so that she will live by the truth.

1 JOHN 1:5–6

Teach _____ to steer clear of any music that smacks of sexual impurity or obscenity, choosing instead to sing and make music in his heart to you.

EPHESIANS 5:3–4, 19

Help _____ to tune her ear to wisdom and concentrate on understanding the message behind each song she hears. Let her cry out for insight so that she will understand what it means to fear the Lord and gain the knowledge of God.

PROVERBS 2:2–5

Strengthen _____ so that when others refuse to put up with sound doctrine and decide to listen to the music that says what their itching ears want to hear, he will keep his ears tuned to hear the truth.

2 TIMOTHY 4:3–4

Let _____ sing for joy to you, Lord, extolling you with music and song. Soften her heart so that she can hear your voice and not be led astray by those who do not know your ways.   Psalm 95:1–2, 7–10

In a generation that has closed its ears and finds your word offensive, prompt _____ to take off his worldly head-phones and open his ears to your voice. Let him listen to you and take delight in your message.   Jeremiah 6:10

Whether _____ turns to the right or to the left, be the voice in her ears, showing her exactly which way to walk—even in the aisles of an online music store.   Isaiah 30:21

As _____ chooses the music he wants to listen to, let him be led by the Holy Spirit. Let him reject music that promotes the desires of his sinful nature: sexual immorality, impure thoughts, hostility, angry outbursts, selfish ambition, and the like, choosing instead to value music that promotes genuine love, peace, kindness, and self-control.

Galatians 5:16–22

Work in _____'s heart so that she will stop loving this evil world and all that it offers. Show her that the world and its music—which is filled with lust, greed, and pride—will fade away, but as she does your will, she will live forever.

1 John 2:15–17

Shield _____ from vulgar and violent music; instead, let the loud noises of singing, shouting, and blasting horns that he hears come from songs of joy because of you.

PSALM 98:4–6

Protect _____'s hearing from being damaged by loud decibels so that she will have ears to hear what your Spirit says.

REVELATION 2:7

Let _____ choose music that promotes life, and let him listen to your voice and hold fast to you.

DEUTERONOMY 30:19–20

CHAPTER 22

Praying for Protection from Drugs

*Don't you realize that whatever you choose to obey
becomes your master? You can choose sin, which leads to death,
or you can choose to obey God and receive his approval.*
ROMANS 6:16 NLT

One of our good friends is the father of four very athletic, outgoing, and fun-loving kids. Their house — if you can find it behind all of the cars and bikes parked in the driveway — is almost always full of teens. There is not much about teenage life that our friend has not seen or heard, and when it comes to knowing what's what, he has a simple but effective parenting motto:

Trust — but verify.

Trust is a vital ingredient in the parent-teen relationship. We should trust our kids — until they give us a reason not to. And when *that* happens, when something happens to rock that trust, we need to kick into "verification mode" right away — particularly when our parental radar says that our kids may be involved with something as potentially dangerous as drugs.

Sometimes verification can be as easy as making a phone call to another parent or having a heart-to-heart talk with your teen. Sometimes, though, the process can be much more difficult. I know one mom whose daughter repeatedly denied that she had had anything to do with drugs. The mother's suspicions persisted, though, and finally — not knowing what else to do — she bought a drug test. Even before the results were in, the girl broke down and admitted to smoking pot. As much as she hated to confront the truth, this mom says that knowing what her family was up against — and being able to get her daughter the help she needed — was infinitely better than living with the constant burden of distrust.

If you suspect that your teen is doing drugs, don't ignore your concerns for lack of proof. And don't assume that just because your kids go to a Christian school, or because they're involved in your church, or because they hang out with a clean-cut crowd, that they will not be exposed to or tempted by marijuana and other drugs. Illegal drugs are everywhere, and I'm probably not telling you anything you don't already know when I say that there are plenty of kids — and a jaw-dropping number of parents — who think that recreational drug use is "no big deal."

That's exactly what my friend Katherine's son Matthew thought. "Everybody," he said, was smoking pot — and it was no big deal.

Thankfully, Katherine didn't see it that way ...

Katherine looked across the master bedroom to where her son Matt sat in the old, familiar recliner. He was a handsome six-foot-two, 225-pound athlete — and he was crying like a baby.

"I can't go back to school," he cried. "Please—you've got to help me."

Katherine felt as though her heart would break. A year ago, her son had asked to be homeschooled, but she had dismissed his request. They had moved to their neighborhood because of its excellent public school system, and she and her husband, Rick, figured that their kids—all of whom had grown up studying the Bible, listening to Christian music, and attending Christ-centered summer camps—would be "salt and light" among their peers.

From the start, Matt had struggled to fit in. A gifted athlete, he competed in sports—but never really wanted to win, since he feared it would hurt his opponent. Even as a young child, Matt had been more concerned for the welfare of others than he was for himself, and in the self-absorbed arena of high school life, he was an enigma. Katherine would never have thought that you could have too big a heart, but—in the world's eyes at least—her oldest son apparently did.

Matt finally began hanging out with some of his fellow athletes. Noting their nice haircuts and even nicer manners, Katherine was glad that Matt had such a strong group of friends. They seemed to be good students—the kind of kids who, Katherine thought, were not likely to get into any real trouble.

A single phone call shattered that illusion. Katherine was driving home from her job as a volunteer counselor with a local pregnancy center when her cell phone rang. She picked it up—and learned that Matt had been spotted with several other kids, doing drugs at three o'clock in the morning the previous weekend.

Life became a blur. What on earth, Katherine wondered, had Matthew been doing out in the middle of the night? Anxious about where it might lead—but needing to know the truth—she purchased a drug test. When she and her husband, Rick, gave it to Matt that night, their fears were confirmed: Matt had been smoking pot.

Katherine and Rick prayed for guidance. Not usually given to making sudden moves, Rick found himself agreeing with Katherine that something had to be done—and fast. There were too many parents in their circle of friends who had grown-up children for whom high school drug use had turned into much more than a relatively short-lived experiment. Several of these kids—many from strong Christian homes—were either still in and out of rehab centers, or living on the streets.

They decided to take Matthew to see a Christian counselor.

"Matthew is a binge drinker who smokes pot about four times a week," the counselor told them. "He's been doing this for about a year, as he and his friends look for ways to deal with peer pressure."

Matthew had gotten the drugs from another athlete—an academically gifted kid whose basketball skills had made him a star on the court and drawn the attention of several college scouts. Matt was, he said, just days away from purchasing some cocaine from the ballplayer, in addition to the marijuana.

"Please," Matthew said again, "don't make me go back to school. I can't take the pressure."

The counselor recommended a couple of drug treatment centers—residential facilities where Matthew could go to regain his footing. After doing some research, Katherine and Rick opted to send him to a place called Capstone, a small

Christ-centered facility geared to helping young men overcome substance abuse and other personal problems.[1]

Within a week, Matthew's bags were packed. Knowing that they would be saying good-bye for three long months, Katherine and the younger children wept as they watched Rick load the suitcases into the car. Visitation was limited to three hours every Sunday — and Matthew would be living in another state! Not only that, but he would be celebrating Thanksgiving, Christmas, and his eighteenth birthday without his family!

Still, Katherine knew it was the right thing to do. Encouraged by a passage from Oswald Chambers' book *My Utmost for His Highest*, she reminded herself that prayer is not preparation for greater works; prayer *is* the greater work.[2] She resolved to pray for Matthew every day and to use every tool at her disposal — from intercessory prayer services at church to websites that accepted prayer requests — to keep her concerns before the Lord.

These are some of the prayers she prayed:

- Let Matthew persevere under this trial, and when all this is behind him, reward him with your crown of life.[3]
- Cause Matthew to come to his senses so that he can escape the trap that Satan has set for him. Work in his heart, and let him believe your truth.[4]
- Help me to remember that when I am afraid, you promise to be with me and to uphold me and give me strength.[5]

---

1. For more information on Capstone, please see the appendix in the back of this book.
2. See Oswald Chambers, *My Utmost for His Highest*, ed. James Reimann (1935; updated edition; Grand Rapids: Discovery House, 1992), October 17 entry.
3. James 1:12.   4. 2 Timothy 2:25–26.   5. Isaiah 41:10.

As Katherine continued to pray—often singing to the Lord through her tears—God went to work on her heart. "You are still trying to hang on to Matthew's problem," her pastor said gently. "You are still trying to control what happens. Try praying with your palms held open, and really release your son to God."

Katherine did so, and she felt the burden of Matthew's addiction—and of his future—lift from her shoulders. Jesus' words in Matthew 22:21—that we should "give to Caesar what is Caesar's, and to God what is God's"—confirmed what the Holy Spirit had whispered to her heart: Matthew belonged to the Lord. Katherine could trust God to take care of her son.

Prayer Principle

Praying with your palms open—
and truly releasing your teen to God—
frees you from the burden of being in control.

Meanwhile, she and Rick found themselves learning volumes about substance abuse, and the puzzle pieces of Matthew's life began fitting together. "Most drug addicts and alcoholics are deep, sensitive people with big hearts," Katherine says. "They feel pain so much deeper than most people."

As if to underscore these words, the Capstone director had a message for Matthew when the time came for him to graduate from the program. "Boy," he said, putting his hands on Matt's shoulders, "you've got a lot of lion and a lot of lamb in you. You are a special man—and God made you for a purpose."

For the first time in his life, Matthew truly believed those words.

More than a year has passed since Matthew left Capstone. He completed his high school degree, worked on staff at a Christian ranch geared to serving teens, and is eyeing a career in Christian counseling. Best of all, he has remained drug and alcohol free. (The basketball playing drug dealer, on the other hand, wound up going to prison instead of to college.)

And Matthew isn't the only one whose life has changed. As the first of their friends to openly acknowledge a child's drug problem, Rick and Katherine now host a weekly support group for parents whose teens are struggling with addictions. God has given them an understanding and a compassion for teens—and, even more, for parents—that they say they never would have had, were it not for Matthew.

"When we're going through a struggle," Katherine says, "it's hard to believe that God is working out something for our good and his glory. But I've learned that as I let go and let God be active in my life, I open my heart to the potential blessings of *every* circumstance—even something as painful as what our family went through."

And—as impossible as it may sound—Katherine maintains that she would not trade her family's experience for anything.

Poised for Prayer

Katherine told me that one of the main reasons they chose the Capstone program rather than a strictly medical treatment facility is that she and Rick are convinced that drug addiction is a spiritual issue. Drug use and the lie that doing drugs will help you "fit in" with your peers are tools that the devil uses in his ongoing battle to destroy our kids.

I completely agree—and yet, when it comes to praying specifically about drug use, parents can face a tough challenge. The Bible doesn't include any verses that talk about pot, cocaine, or other drugs; if we want to pray scripturally, where do we begin?

We can, I think, take a two-pronged approach. We can pray for protection from Satan's lies, and ask God to help our teens see and be drawn to the Truth. We can also pray against the power of addiction.

Teens are all about wanting freedom. If you asked your teen if he or she wanted to become a slave, you'd probably be rewarded with an eyeball roll or—to borrow a quote from one of our daughters—with a somewhat scornful "What?" Nobody in his or her right mind would sign up for a life of slavery, and yet each time our kids give themselves over to drugs or alcohol, even to a small degree, they are exchanging some of their freedom for bondage. The worse the problem gets, the tighter the chains hold.

The only way for our teens to break the power of drug addiction—and for that matter, the only way that any of us can break the power of any sin—is to surrender themselves completely to God, giving him control of their thoughts, their actions, and their lives. When we realize how much is at stake, it becomes easier to pray specifically and with conviction.

It's a battle, to be sure—and it can be doubly hard when you feel as though you are praying and fighting against a world whose viewpoint is often radically different from your own. But don't be discouraged. Rather, put your trust in God, and ask him to give you wisdom and strength. The world may be full of lies, but you *will* overcome—because, as the Scriptures remind us, "Greater is He who is in you than he who is in the world."[1]

---

1. 1 John 4:4 NASB.

Prayers You Can Use

Heavenly Father,

Show _____ that as he gives himself completely to you, drugs can no longer be his master. Do not let him be enslaved to any kind of sin; rather, set him free by your grace.

ROMANS 6:14

Put people in _____'s path who will gently teach her. Cause her to come to her senses so that she will believe the truth and escape from the trap of drugs and lies that Satan has used to hold her captive.   2 TIMOTHY 2:25–26

Shield _____ from the weapon of drugs. Banish terror from his life, and give him peace.   ISAIAH 54:13, 17

When _____'s peers experiment with drug use, do not let her conform to their pattern; rather, transform her life by renewing her mind so that she will want to do what pleases you.   ROMANS 12:1–2

Demolish any strongholds of lying, rebellion, and drug use in _____'s life. Remove anything that gets in the way of his knowledge of you, and cause his thought life to be obedient to Christ.   2 CORINTHIANS 10:4–5

Help _____ to see the truth—that people who use drugs and who push them on her are bent on stealing, killing, and destroying. Prompt her to turn to you, knowing that your plan is to give her a full, abundant life.

JOHN 10:10

Remind _____ that his body is your temple. Things may look as though they are in ruins now, but help him not to be afraid. Fill your temple with your glory, and bring peace to his life, so that the future will be greater than the past.   HAGGAI 1:9, 2:5–9

Help _____ to persevere when she faces trials, relying on your strength instead of on drugs. Equip her to stand during times of testing so that she can receive the crown of life that you have promised to those who love you.

JAMES 1:12

Do not let _____ blame you for his actions; instead, teach him that temptation comes from his own evil desires. Keep _____ from giving in to those desires, since all they will do is lead to sin and death. Don't let him be deceived.   JAMES 1:13–16

Protect _____ from the snare of drugs that others lay out for her. Shield her from things such as date rape drugs and other traps set by evildoers.   PSALM 141:9

Open _____'s eyes so that he can see that drugs are a way that may seem right, but in the end they lead to death.
PROVERBS 14:12

Set _____ free, and help her to stand firm. Do not let her be burdened by a yoke of slavery to drugs or to any other evil.
GALATIANS 5:1

CHAPTER 23

Praying for Sin to Be Exposed

*You may be sure that
your sin will find you out.*

NUMBERS 32:23

"If my kid is doing something wrong, Lord, please let him get caught."

Believe it or not, almost every parent I surveyed as I began writing this book said that the "let my kids get caught" prayer— a parent's version of Numbers 32:23—was at or near the top of their list. Judging by the emails I received, parents want their teens to get caught even more than they want them to finish their chores, say no to drugs, and stop wrecking the car.

I don't mind telling you that I was somewhat surprised— and impressed—by this vigilante mind-set. Like it or not, we live in a world where many parents cover for their kids and do everything they can to minimize the consequences of bad decisions—whether it means staying up all night to finish a procrastinator's science project or hiring a lawyer to get charges dropped against a teen who drove home drunk. Who knew that there were so many of us who would actually let our kids pay the piper?

Sharon is a dear friend of mine who says that she hates to pray the "let my kids get caught" prayer, because every time she does, God answers. One night, for example, her teenage son kissed a girl, figuring that Sharon would never know. Unbeknownst to the young Romeo, the girl went straight home and emailed all the details to her older sister, who forwarded the missive to one of her best friends—who just happened to be Sharon's oldest daughter! Within twenty-four hours, the email had made its way to Sharon's in-box—and "Romeo" found himself with some serious explaining to do!

I'm no statistician, but according to my very unscientific calculations, pretty much everybody's teen has done something wrong. If you are one of those parents who has prayed the "let them get caught" prayer, my guess is that God has been faithful to answer it. If, on the other hand, you haven't tried this one yet, consider yourself warned. The kiss-and-tell email was relatively painless compared to what many parents find themselves facing when God lets their kids get caught.

Prayer Principle

When you ask God to let your kids get caught,
be prepared. The answer to your prayer
can be hard—but God's power, wisdom, and grace
will get you through even the darkest night.

Sally is a wise Christian woman whose kids are enough older than mine to make her one of my main "go-to gals" when I need answers and advice. Her children all love the Lord, but raising them has not been without its share of heartache. Like many of the godly parents I've talked with, Sally wanted—and even expected—to have a poster-perfect Christian family. But then she had teens ...

"Honey, are you ready to go? The game starts in forty-five minutes!"

Living in a college town, Sally and her husband, Rob, had become ardent fans of the university's athletic program. They had season tickets for football and basketball and almost never missed a home game. In addition to providing some good, clean entertainment, attending the games—and cheering their heads off—provided a way for Sally and Rob to connect with their teens, who loved sports every bit as much as they did. Having just sent her older daughter off to college, Sally was all too aware that Allison, their tenth-grader, would soon be gone, and she wanted to make the most of the remaining time they had together.

"Just a second, Rob," Sally replied. "I think there's something wrong with the dishwasher."

Sure enough, the appliance was overflowing—and with the clock ticking down to tip-off, a decision had to be made. "I'll call the plumber," Sally volunteered. "You and Allison go on ahead. I'll try to meet up with you at halftime."

Fortunately, the plumber was nearby. He quickly fixed the problem, and Sally followed him out to the driveway, thinking that if she hurried, she might be able to catch the end of the game. Her thoughts were interrupted, however, when her next-door neighbor, Ben, came out to quiet his dog.

"Sorry about the barking," Ben said. "I guess Trixie just wanted us to know that you had a repairman here."

"That's OK," Sally answered. "I appreciate knowing that she's on patrol."

"Well, speaking of being on patrol," Ben began, "I didn't want to say anything, but I think there's something you need to know."

Sally felt her heart skip a beat. She and Rob had just returned from a long weekend away—had there been a burglary in the neighborhood?

"I hate to be the one to tell you this, but while you were gone, Allison had some friends over."

"What? How many friends?" Sally hoped she hadn't heard correctly. Allison had been staying with a young Christian couple who had agreed to host her for the weekend. She wasn't supposed to be at home while Rob and Sally were gone.

"I don't know—maybe a hundred or so."

"What?!"

"I don't think she meant for it to get out of hand. Allison is a good girl. We offered to help her get rid of everyone, but she said she could handle it."

"Mm-hmm," Sally said, her thoughts now far from the basketball game. "Well, thanks for telling me."

Later that night, when Rob and Allison came home, Sally confronted her daughter with what she had learned. The story spilled out—and the longer it got, the worse it became.

Sally and Rob had given Allison permission to spend the night at a girlfriend's house one of the nights they were gone. Instead of going there, the girls decided it would be more fun to invite a few friends to gather at Allison's house. Thanks to the teenage network of cell phones and instant messaging, what began as a small get-together quickly turned into a full-fledged bash, attracting a huge crowd of boys and girls, many of whom were drinking and smoking. Several girls wound up spending the night at Allison's house—without any adult supervision and without their parents' knowledge.

Sally felt sick to her stomach. In addition to betraying her parents' trust, Allison had deceived her babysitters, endangered her friends, and compromised her own integrity. Everyone in the community knew that Sally and Rob were Christians—what sort of message did it send when one of the biggest, baddest parties of the year was at their house?

"It was awful," Sally said later, as she shared the story with me. "Of course, Allison was grounded. And she had to go to the parents of all the girls who had spent the night at our house and write them a letter to personally apologize for initiating the get-together and for being complicit in the deception. When she finally woke up to the fact that she had put her girlfriends' reputations—and even their lives—in danger, she truly felt terrible. It was a learning experience, to say the least."

When I asked Sally if I could use her story in this book, she got Allison's permission before saying yes. While neither of them want to dwell on the mistakes that were made, both mother and daughter acknowledge that, thanks to God's grace, what started out as a very bad choice turned into an opportunity for learning, growing, and changing.

"Had our dishwasher not started overflowing," Sally said, "who knows when—or even if—we would have found out about the party. But one thing I can say for certain is that if you pray for your teen to be found out when they do something they shouldn't—when they break the rules, lie, drink, or go somewhere they shouldn't go—it is amazing how faithfully God answers that prayer.

"And," Sally concluded, "even though it's sometimes painful to find out your teen's transgressions and have to deal with the consequences, it is *so* much better than never knowing."

Poised for Prayer

As you might imagine, it wasn't easy for Sally to share her story with me. Nobody wants to talk about the big bloopers in their family. But I am grateful for her honesty and candor, because there is so much about her story that can fill us with hope and encouragement. I hope you saw what I saw.

For one thing, Sally and her husband are godly parents. Their love for the Lord colors pretty much everything about their family life, and if you didn't know better, you might believe that they *are* poster-perfect. If you look around at families in your church and think that other people "have it all together," think again. Everybody struggles. We *all* fall short.

Next, did you notice what Sally and Rob did when God answered their prayers? When Allison got caught, they didn't try to cover up her sin or blame someone else. It would have been very easy—and I imagine very tempting—to point the finger at the kids who "crashed" Allison's party, but Sally and Rob didn't go there. Instead, they held their daughter accountable, using the experience as a teaching tool for lessons in such areas as personal responsibility and the importance of confession. We can learn from their example as we deal openly with our kids' mistakes and see them as opportunities for growth.

And finally, their story underscores the beauty of God's faithfulness and grace. When we ask him to let our kids get caught, we can do so, knowing that he isn't going to hang them out to dry. He loves them way too much for that. He will let them get caught—but he will also catch them as they fall. God is in the restoration business, and as parents, we can work hand in hand with him to get our teens back on their feet.

Remember Joseph—the guy with the technicolor dreamcoat? He was a teen when his brothers sold him into slavery and faked his death. Years later, after Joseph grew up and masterminded one of history's most successful disaster relief programs, he confronted his siblings. Instead of harboring bitterness and anger, though, he pointed to the evidence of God's handiwork. "You intended to harm me," Joseph said to his brothers in Genesis 50:20, "but God intended it for good to accomplish what is now being done, the saving of many lives."

When our kids do bad things—and they will—let's not give in to doubt or discouragement. Instead, let's adjust our perspective and look for God's divine fingerprints, trusting in his promise to take even the darkest situation and use it to bring about something good.

Prayers You Can Use

Heavenly Father,

You see everything that _____ does. Open my eyes to the things that I need to see and know about my son, and give me the wisdom and the courage to deal with the situation when he is caught doing wrong.   PROVERBS 15:3

_____'s sins—even the secret ones—are spread out before you. When she stumbles, teach her to make the most of her time and to grow in wisdom.   PSALM 90:8, 12

Cause _____ to renounce his secret and shameful ways. Do not let him use deception or do anything that would distort your word.   2 CORINTHIANS 4:2

Let _____ have nothing to do with the fruitless deeds of darkness, but rather expose them, realizing that it is shameful even to mention what the disobedient do in secret. Shine the light of your presence into her life.

EPHESIANS 5:11–14

When _____ is caught in sin, have mercy on him. Wash away his iniquity, and make him clean. Create a pure heart in him, and make him willing to obey you.

PSALM 51:1–2, 10–12

Lord, if you kept a record of our sins, who could ever survive? Prompt _____ to take hold of the forgiveness you offer, and let her learn to fear you and put her hope in your word.

PSALM 130:3–5

Give _____ back what he has lost to the army of locusts that has tried to destroy him, and let him never again be disgraced like this.

JOEL 2:25–26

Let _____ look to you and be radiant, that her face may never be covered with shame.

PSALM 34:5

When _____ thinks that the darkness will hide him, remind him that darkness is as light to you, and that you are the one who makes the night shine like the day. Search him and know his heart. Turn your spotlight on any offensive words, thoughts, or behaviors in his life, and lead him in the way everlasting.

PSALM 139:11–12, 23–24

Show _____ that she has been chosen by you, that she belongs to you, and that her job is to declare your praises. Let her abstain from sinful desires and live such a good life among her friends and classmates that they will see her good deeds and glorify you.

1 PETER 2:9–12

In a world where many teens hate the light because they want to sin in the darkness, cause _____ to do what is right and come into the light gladly, so that everyone can see that he is doing what you want. JOHN 3:20–21

Remind _____ that when she sins against you, her sin will find her out. NUMBERS 32:23

PART 5

PRAYING
for Your **TEEN'S**
FUTURE

CHAPTER 24

Praying for Education, Career, Marriage, and More

No eye has seen,
no ear has heard,
no mind has conceived
what God has prepared for those who love him.
1 Corinthians 2:9

A funny thing happened on the way to the publisher. I have always prayed for my kids, but as I sought to widen my range and discover prayer topics and related Scriptures that would be relevant to an audience beyond my own family, my own need for those far-ranging prayers began to expand dramatically. While I was working on the chapter about teenage drivers, for instance, one daughter called with the news that the car had two flat tires—and she was two hours away from home. Dabbling in the "teachable heart" chapter, another teen landed on a sports team where the coach's motivational style and player-placement strategies revealed huge holes in our humility. And in case you thought I was standing on a mighty high soapbox when I wrote about the need for modesty in our teens' attire, I have to confess that, as I was writing some of those prayers, God not so gently reminded me of the time that my daughter and two of her friends went to a rock concert dressed in skimpy shirts they had made themselves—using an untold number of staples and shimmery fabric ransacked from a neighbor's nativity set!

Truth be told, during the time it took to research and write this book, my husband and I wound up praying our way through almost every topic found in the table of contents. I even found myself wondering whether God—in that God-like way of his—allowed some specific challenges to manifest themselves in our family just to remove any lingering threads of self-sufficiency, pride, and judgmental attitudes I might have tried to hang on to had I not found myself in the parenting gutter so many times.

That being said, I realize that there are scads of other issues I haven't even touched on in these pages, ranging from academic struggles and sibling relationships to pressure points such as pregnancy and abortion to helping teens find their way when their landscape changes due to things such as divorce, a move, and even the death of a close friend or family member.

To find Scripture verses to undergird prayer needs such as these, consider using a concordance and start by looking up words that relate to your concern. Words such as "comfort" and "strength" will yield a rich harvest of promises you can pray on behalf of a hurting teen; other choices—such as "wisdom," "discernment," and "diligence"—offer valuable insight into praying for those types of needs. You can use your own prayer journal to record the prayer verses you find. Try picking a few of your favorite Scriptures, either from the preceding chapters or from your own "gold mining" efforts, and commit them to memory so that you will be ready to fight the battle on behalf of your teen as needs arise.

When it comes to praying about your teen's future — whether you need wisdom in selecting the right college, peace about a chosen career path, or guidance and protection during the seasons of dating, engagement, and marriage — try looking up words such as "future," "plans," and "purpose." As I pray for my own teens, I love to remind them of God's promise in Jeremiah 29:11 – 13:

> "For I know the plans I have for you," declares the LORD, "plans to prosper you and not to harm you, plans to give you hope and a future. Then you will call upon me and come and pray to me, and I will listen to you. You will seek me and find me when you seek me with all your heart."

Not only does God have specific and generous plans for our teens, but he has promised to listen to them and to be found by them as they press on to know him better. What a beautiful launching pad for a parent's prayers!

When I wrote *Praying the Scriptures for Your Children*, I quoted pastor and author Jack Hayford, who says that prayer is a "partnership of the redeemed child of God working hand in hand with God toward the realization of his redemptive purposes on earth."[1] As you look ahead toward your teen's future — toward his or her God-given purpose in life — can you think of anything more encouraging than knowing that when you pray about things like educational prospects, ministry opportunities, and marriage, you are slipping your hand

---

1. Jodie Berndt, *Praying the Scriptures for Your Children* (Grand Rapids: Zondervan, 2001), 17.

into Almighty God's hand and inviting him to bring about all that he has planned?

Obviously, there are no rules or formulas to dictate how we should pray for our teens, but I want to offer a few principles that have helped to shape my own prayers for their future. When it comes to my kids' education, for instance, I am asking God to place a hedge of protection around their hearts and emotions so that they will not be drawn to any colleges that are not on his heavenly radar for them. I pray that their guidance counselors will have wisdom and discernment and that the Lord will bring older teens and young adults into their lives who will open their eyes to schools that they might not have considered. I also pray for my husband, Robbie, and me, that our preconceived ideas about colleges—everything from academic rankings to social and spiritual environments—would bow in submission to God's perspective on the subject.

In terms of an eventual job or career path, I love the wisdom my friend Susan offers. As we seek to prepare our kids for what lies ahead, Susan says that "God's job is to call them; our job is simply to equip them for whatever he has planned." With this goal in mind, she and her husband, John, sought to give their five children the skills and the perspectives they would need to dine with homeless people as well as with kings. "I don't know whether God will call my kids to work in a soup kitchen or as the United States ambassador to the Court of St. James," she once told me. "I want them to be ready—and willing—to do whatever God has planned."

Reading Susan's annual family letter this year, I couldn't help but think that it was a good thing that she had parented—and prayed—the way she did. Her kids are now grown up, married, and living all over the map—including in England, just a stone's throw from the Court of St. James! Through their family lives, business pursuits, and ministry opportunities, every one of them is serving the Lord and accomplishing his purposes—drawing from a deep well of parental prayers and preparation.

Prayer Principle

God's job is to call our teens.
Our job is to equip them to respond.

On the subject of marriage, it's never too early to start praying for your teen's eventual spouse and for their marriage itself. This arena represents a wonderful opportunity to practice praying specifically. Rather than praying that your teen will marry a particular *person*, however, allow things like *character traits* and *personal attibutes* to shape your prayers. One of my friends—whose own parents are divorced—prays that her teens will marry men and women who come from unbroken homes. Another friend has put things such as honesty, purity, and a good sense of humor on her prayer list for her kids' eventual mates. My own prayers tend to center around husbands and wives who have a passion for Christ—loving him with all their heart, soul, mind, and strength[1]—and who know the blessings and joy that accompany strong family relationships and a commitment to honoring your parents.[2]

In all of these areas—education, career paths, ministry opportunities, and marriage—perhaps the best prayer we can

1. Mark 12:30.   2. Exodus 20:12.

pray for our teens is that God's presence will go with them. God's charge in Joshua 1:9 — that the Israelites would "be strong and courageous" and not terrified or discouraged, since he had promised to be with them — might offer encouragement to a teen or a young adult as he heads off on a missions trip or into a new job, but it proves an even more potent salve when applied to the heart of an anxious parent! When my twentysomething brother, David, and his young bride Cherie moved to China last year, the knowledge that God had called them to go — and that he had promised to be with them — was probably the only thing that kept our families from wrapping ourselves around their legs at the airport!

Finally, when you consider your teen's future and look at his or her interests and abilities, remember the wisdom couched in 1 Samuel 16:7 — that God doesn't always see things the same way that people do. When our family took a surfing vacation in Central America, Hillary — then sixteen — didn't brush her hair for a week. She washed it, so I didn't complain; I just put it down to some sort of teenage "self-expression." But then I looked around at the locals, and realized that Hillary — the only one of us who speaks Spanish — blended into the laid-back culture beautifully. And when we met an American seminary graduate who holds church services in an open-air restaurant, she was entranced. Hillary loved the fellow's outreach style — and as I observed her during our trip, I found myself thanking God for the way he had put her together. With her tousled blonde hair and coconut-ringed fingers, Hillary had been equipped to go into places where hair dryer–dependent folks like me never could!

Poised for Prayer

I don't know where you are right now or what decisions your family is facing, but I am confident of this: *God loves your teen, and he has a wonderful plan for his or her life.* As you look back on all the ways that God has answered your prayers—from the days even before your son or daughter was born until right now, when God is continuing the good work that he has already started[1]—take a few moments to thank him. Look back over his track record of faithfulness. You may not know what the future holds, but you know who holds the future.

Go ahead and put up that Ebenezer stone—marking the fact that "thus far" the Lord has helped you—and expect great and glorious things in the days ahead![2]

> LORD, I have heard of your fame;
>   I stand in awe of your deeds, O LORD.
> Renew them in our day,
>   in our time make them known.

HABAKKUK 3:2

---

1. Philippians 1:6.   2. 1 Samuel 7:12.

Prayers You Can Use

Heavenly Father,

Let _____ be glad for all that you are planning for him. Help him to be patient in trouble and to be ready to pray about everything.   ROMANS 12:12

As _____ weighs the choices that are before her, let her be filled with knowledge and depth of insight, that she may be able to discern what is best and be pure and blameless until Jesus comes again. In her college, her career, and her marriage, let her be filled with the fruit of righteousness that comes through Jesus, so that everything she does will bring glory to your name.   PHILIPPIANS 1:9–11

Remind _____ that you know the plans you have for him—plans to prosper him and not to harm him, plans to give him hope and a future. Cause him to turn to you for wisdom and guidance in all things, and listen to his prayers.
                    JEREMIAH 29:11–12

As _____ grows and becomes more independent, teach her to trust in you with all her heart. Do not let her depend on her own understanding, but cause her to seek your will in all that she does, and direct her paths.

                    PROVERBS 3:5–6

*When _____ comes up against a big decision —
whether it is a career choice, a marriage partner, or something
else — do not let him look at the things that human
beings look at. Instead, cause him to see the world through
your eyes and to respond to people and circumstances with
your wisdom and your love.* 1 SAMUEL 16:7

*Fill _____ with the knowledge of your will through all
spiritual wisdom and understanding, that she may live a life
worthy of you and please you in every way.*

COLOSSIANS 1:9 – 10

*Enable _____ to support and provide for his family, so
that no one can accuse him of denying his faith or behaving
worse than an unbeliever would.* 1 TIMOTHY 5:8

*Teach _____ to make the most of her time, so that she
may grow in wisdom.* PSALM 90:12

*Do not let _____ be arrogant or put his hope in money,
which is so uncertain. Instead, cause him to put his trust in
you and to enjoy all that you have provided. Let him be rich
in good deeds, being generous and always willing to share, so
that he can take hold of the life that is truly life.*

1 TIMOTHY 6:17 – 19

Place a hedge of protection around _____ and all that she has, so that nothing will harm her and so that she will not be drawn to anything that is not from you. Bless the work of her hands, so that she will prosper in all that she does.   JOB 1:10

When _____ meets and falls in love with the one he will marry, let their relationship be marked by patience, kindness, humility, selflessness, truthfulness, and joy. Let their love never fail.   1 CORINTHIANS 13:4–8

Whatever _____'s hand finds to do, let her work at it with all her heart, knowing that she is ultimately working for you and not for human masters.

COLOSSIANS 3:23

Do immeasurably more in _____'s life than all we could ever ask or imagine. Display your power in his life, and let all that he does bring glory to you, Lord God.

EPHESIANS 3:20–21

Recommended Resources

I am grateful to the following authors and organizations for all the ways their work has encouraged and equipped our family and contributed to my understanding of some of the issues teens grapple with today. While there are countless other resources available to today's parents, I recommend these few in the hope that they will challenge and inspire you to follow Jesus Christ in your parenting and in your prayer life. In addition, many of the parents who shared their stories for this book are available as a resource to you. You may contact them through me at Zondervan.

Books and Magazines

Barnes, Bob. *Preparing Your Child for Dating.* Grand Rapids: Zondervan 1998.

Channing L. Bete, Co., Inc., *About Anorexia Nervosa* (1996) and *About Bulimia Nervosa* (1997). South Deerfield, Mass. To order a copy of these booklets, call 1-800-628-7733.

Courtney, Vicki. *Your Girl: Raising a Godly Daughter in an Ungodly World.* Nashville: Broadman & Holman 2004.

Luce, Ron. *"It's Only a Tattoo" and Other Myths Teens Believe.* Colorado Springs: Cook, 2006.

Sheets, Dutch. *Intercessory Prayer: Discover How God Can Use Your Prayers to Move Heaven and Earth.* Ventura, Calif.: Regal, 1997.

Tripp, Paul David. *Age of Opportunity: A Biblical Guide to Parenting Teens.* Phillipsburg, N.J.: P & R, 2001.

White, Joe, and Jim Weidemann, eds. *Parents' Guide to the Spiritual Mentoring of Teens: Building Your Child's Faith through the Adolescent Years*. Wheaton, Ill.: Tyndale House, for Focus on the Family, 2001.

Yates, Susan. *And Then I Had Teenagers: Encouragement for Parents of Teens and Preteens*. Grand Rapids: Baker, 2001.

Breakaway (for boys) and *Brio* (for girls) are designed to make Christianity alive and relevant for teens. These glossy magazines feature sports, music, advice columns, humor, people profiles, and much more. Available through Focus on the Family at www.family.org/resources.

Ministries, Camps, and Organizations

Moms in Prayer International (formerly Moms In Touch)
Fern Nichols, president and founder
PO Box 1120
Poway, CA 92074-1120
www.momsinprayer.org

Teaches and equips women to pray for their children and their schools.

Young Life
Denny Rydberg, president
PO Box 520
Colorado Springs, CO 80901-0520
www.younglife.org

A nondenominational Christian ministry reaching teens through weekly club meetings, Bible studies, and camping programs.

Kanakuk Kamps
Joe White, president and owner
1353 Lakeshore Drive
Branson, MO 65616-9470
www.kanakuk.com

Exciting adventures in Christian athletics via summer
camping programs and resort-style family camping.

Pure Excitement
Joe White
1353 Lakeshore Drive
Branson, MO 65616
www.pureexcitement.com

High-energy stadium events designed to equip teens to make
godly choices about love, dating, and sex.

Teen Mania Ministries
Ron Luce, founder and CEO
PO Box 2000
Garden Valley, TX 75771
www.teenmania.org

Equips and trains teens for global evangelism via stadium
events, mission trips, camps, and other activities.

Fellowship of Christian Athletes (FCA)
Les Steckel, president and CEO
8701 Leeds Road
Kansas City, MO 64129
www.fca.org

Evangelism and discipleship targeted toward young athletes
and their coaches.

Remuda Ranch

Ward Keller, founder
Chris Diamond, executive director
One East Apache Street
Wickenburg, AZ 85390
www.remudaranch.com

Offers intensive inpatient programs for girls and women suffering from anorexia, bulimia, and related issues.

Capstone Treatment Center

Adrian Hickmon, executive director
PO Box 8241
Searcy, AR 72145
www.capstonetreatmentcenter.com

A Christ-centered residential treatment facility designed to help young men overcome drug addiction and related problems.

Subject Index